Film ⟷ Video
Terms and Concepts

Steven E. Browne

Focal Press
Boston   London

Focal Handbooks

Arthur Schneider *Electronic Post-Production Terms and Concepts*
Steven E. Browne *Film ⇌ Video Terms and Concepts*

Focal Press is an imprint of Butterworth–Heinemann.

Library of Congress Cataloging-in-Publication Data
Browne, Steven E.
   Film-video terms and concepts / by Steven E. Browne.
      p.   cm.—(Focal handbooks)
   On t.p. arrows point in both directions between "film" and "video".
   ISBN 0-240-80111-3 (pbk.)
   1. Cinematography—Dictionaries.   2. Video tape recorders and recording—Dictionaries.   I. Title.   II. Series.
   TR847.B76   1992   91-33264
   778.5—dc20

British Library Cataloguing-in-Publication Data
Browne, Steven E.
   Film-video terms and concepts.
   I. Title
   791.43
   ISBN 0-240-80111-3

Butterworth–Heinemann
80 Montvale Avenue
Stoneham, MA 02180

10 9 8 7 6 5 4 3 2 1

Printed in the United States of America

To Michele, who makes all things possible.

Acknowledgments

I would like to express my deep appreciation to the many individuals who helped in the preparation of this manuscript—from my extremely supportive family to the many helpful, knowledgeable people that tolerated my experimental comparisons.

The most important person whom I'd like to thank was Ashraf Wasseff, a tremendously gifted and creative professional. He was a great friend.

In addition, I would like to thank Corky O'Hara, Mike Sacks, Annette Hunt, and Archie Hampton for their advice and guidance, as well as the helpful, trusting people at Focal Press, with a special nod to Philip Sutherland.

Finally, there is Michele, my wife, without whom there would be no book in the first place.

Introduction

In spite of the parallel existence of film and video, confusion still exists about the various technical terms and ideas found in the two mediums. This book was written to further the understanding of these powerful systems by drawing comparisons between the two. There are many physical and conceptual aspects of film and video that are strikingly similar. The goal here is to introduce the alternative medium by pointing out the abundant commonalities they possess.

As Figures 1 and 2 demonstrate, film and video follow similar yet individual production and post-production paths. Certainly there are differences, that only certain film takes are printed and that audio is usually recorded on a medium separate from the visual; but both mediums go through the work print or off-line stage, both use audio mixing devices, and both have very powerful influences on their audiences.

Several interesting developments are occurring in the visual industry concerning the melding of these two technologies. Generally speaking, the amount of film production is growing, but the advances in video technologies are being utilized more often. Random-access editing systems have already been used in feature film post-production. Trailers for motion pictures are edited on videotape. Moves are transferred to videotape for viewing on cable, cassettes, and television broadcast. Film titles and opticals are being designed on electronic graphic systems.

Digital audio workstations (DAWs) and multitrack mixing (the film equivalent of *dubbing*) are being embraced by increasing numbers of filmmakers. The visual community is becoming more and more aware of the expanding horizons offered by the electronic world and has become willing to try those methods if there is a cost-effective or creative advantage to be had.

From all this information, a pattern appears to be emerging. Film is often the production medium of choice. Video, with its assorted electronic devices, including audio, is becoming a post-production medium. Figures 3 and 4

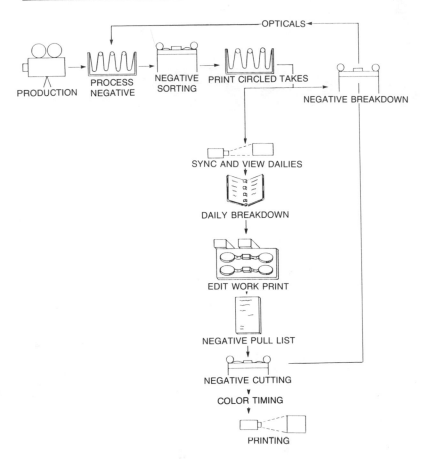

Figure 1   Film negative picture process. The film negative process has been refined over the years, but the basic path has remained a constant.

illustrate two common methods where film is utilized as the production medium and video as the post-production element. These two paths have already been well worn in the television arena.

Also, an interesting observation became apparent as I researched this book. Film is often referred to by industry professionals in *physical* terms, while videotape is described in the abstract. Film is handled, cut, and (regrettably) scratched. Videotape is loaded and previewed and has dropouts. Film length is referred to in feet, videotape in running time. Film can be

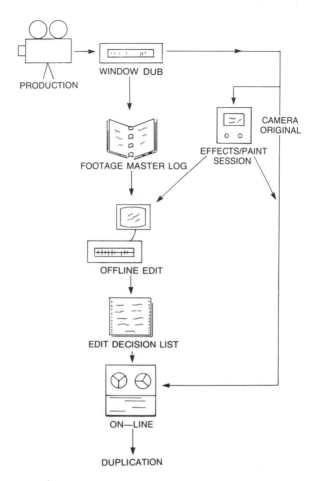

Figure 2 Video picture process.

touched and can be viewed with the unaided eye. Videotape is never touched and is viewed by means of an electronic playback device and a monitor.

In following this thinking, it became apparent that film, being a physical medium, often needs to be experienced. Yet videotape, because it is hidden in cassettes and inside playback devices and only exists as an unrecognizable magnetic signal, needs to be imagined.

These two different concepts have also proved helpful in understanding the two different mediums. There is always a physical process involved with

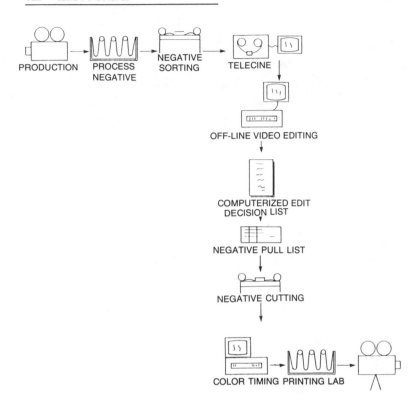

Figure 3 Film production, video post, film finish. More and more, film and video are joining forces. With a properly maintained key-number to time-code reference, film can be edited on video. The time code listing is then converted to key numbers for conforming. Film remains an important release medium, especially in foreign theater as well as broadcasting.

film. With videotape, more often than not, the process is part of an unseen, visualized, electronic system.

If the film and video processes were running in identical yet parallel paths, there would be no need for this text. This is not the case. There are examples in both film and video processes where there are no direct comparisons, where the process in question is unique to that medium; and there are gray areas, where one comparison works as well as another.

Within these pages are readable explanations of the numerous parallel concepts between film and video. The walls are down. All that needs to happen is that the communication continue. This book is a start in the right direction.

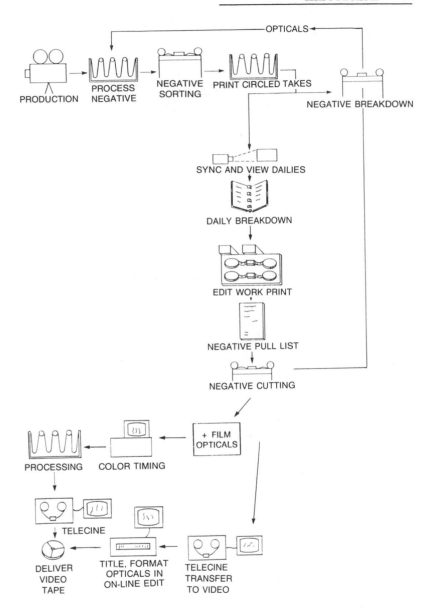

Figure 4 Film production, film post, video deliver. This process can take two turns, depending on whether opticals are being created in film or video. Many television shows are still optically completing their shows so that the telecine transfer can be recorded to any required video format.

NOTATION

There are five symbols used in this text; each has a specific meaning within the confines of this book.

🎥 This symbol indicates a word or concept that is basically film-oriented and is not commonly found around video users.

▭ This symbol indicates a video word or concept that is not generally found around film production.

🎞 This symbol indicates a word that is common to both film and video situations.

⇌ This symbol is used to indicate the equivalent definition of the term in the alternate technology; that is, if the original is a film-oriented word, the symbol denotes the video equivalent and vice versa.

≠ This symbol, used rarely, indicates an explanation of the difference between terms that might seem alike but are used in a completely different manner.

A/B roll

📽 Used in 16-millimeter-film post-production situations when there is an effect (more than one picture on the screen at a time) (Figure 5) or when film is being prepared for processing an answer print.

In 16-millimeter-film post-production, the frame line is too small to allow a hot splice without having the splice appear in the film. This does not present a problem in work-print editing, but when it comes to negative cutting, and subsequent printing, this seam is unacceptable. In order to create an answer print in 16-millimeter, the negative is cut in A/B rolls, that is, in a checkerboard pattern (Figure 6). On the A string of the film is every other scene. The remaining scenes are on the B film string. The two reels are then sent through a printer, creating an answer print and eliminating the visible frame line that occurs when hot splicing 16-millimeter film.

⟻ A/B reels are the video equivalent of A/B rolls; used for an efficient on-line editing session. Many industrial-program producers will build A/B reels using their own editing systems. Where effects are to occur, picture overlaps are on the two separate reels (Figure 7). If mixing is going to occur during the on-line session, these two playbacks can provide up to four source tracks of audio.

☐ An editing system, also called **A/B editing**, that can control more than one playback machine and perform dissolves. In video editing, a dissolve always requires a *from* reel and a *to* reel, even if the two pictures are on the same reel. See also *B roll.*

In most cases, the term *A/B roll* is related to consumer-formats editing systems (VHS, Betamax, 8 millimeter, etc.), three-quarter-inch editing systems, or Betacam news-editing situations. In high-end-industrial and broadcast editing suites, A/B roll capability is assumed. Because so many industrial editing rooms are configured as *cuts only,* the term *A/B rolls* takes on a heightened importance as it indicates that a specific editing bay is capable of making limited effects (dissolves, wipes, and/or keys).

1

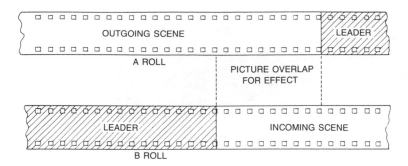

Figure 5   Effects edit A/B. This A/B process is used for 16-millimeter film lab preparation for effects.

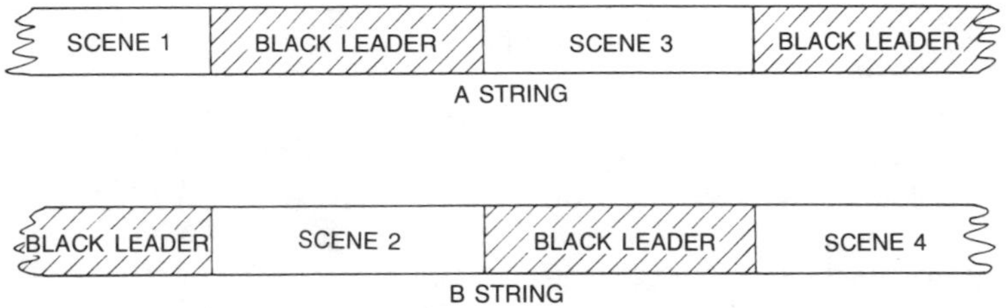

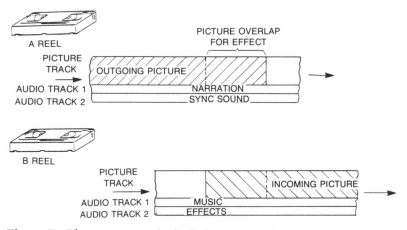

Figure 6   Checkerboard A/B. This A/B preparation is for 16-millimeter lab preparation. Note that there is no overlap between cuts.

Figure 7   Three-quarter-inch checkerboard. A process used by cost-conscious producers. By segment editing onto two synchronous tapes, effects are prepped, and four channels of audio are accessible for a more complicated on-line.

➡ The film equivalent of an A/B roll editing system would be an optical printer, rather than a contact printer.

🎥 **above the line**   The creative costs involved in making a film or television program, which include salaries for the writer, producer, director, actors, and so forth. The opposite of this term is *below the line*, which includes the costs of the technical crew and other, usually fixed, production costs (camera rental, stock, camera crew, etc.).

academy leader

📽 A 12-foot-long section of film with a countdown of descending numbers either in feet or seconds that is placed at the front of a film reel. The academy leader is designed to protect the head of the film and to provide a place for reel identification and synchronization marks. The academy leader that is found on videotape usually originates from a film that has been transferred to tape. See also *leader*.

➡ The video comparison would be a *slate* combined with a countdown. Almost all production and edited material is visually slated with some sort of identification. Many producers also record a countdown at the head of video program material. Most video editing facilities develop a unique, creative countdown that is recorded at the beginning of programs edited at their company.

Academy of Motion Picture Arts and Sciences (AMPAS)

📽 A nonprofit, professional, honorary organization dedicated to furthering the arts and sciences of motion picture production. This is the organization that created and is responsible for the Academy Award ceremonies, known as the Oscars.

➡ There are two organizations that parallel the Academy. First would be the National Association of Broadcasters (NAB), which is focused on furthering the technical and business aspects of television. A less technically orientated group is the National Association of Television Arts and Sciences, an umbrella group of television professionals that is responsible for the awards ceremony known as the Emmys and that provides education, funding, and other academic services to the community.

acetate

📽 A commonly used base for film stock, which is coated with light-sensitive emulsion. An alternative and less used base is polyester. Nitrate was the base used long ago, but it was extremely flammable. See also *base*.

➡ Mylar is used for the base for videotape. This base is coated with an oxide, the material that stores the electronic information used to create the video image.

🎥 **action**

    1. The vital point of attention within each frame; can be an individual or individuals, inanimate objects, and so forth.

    2. Command traditionally given to begin a take.

additive color system

☐ A color system that uses three primary light colors—red, green, and blue—to create the rest of the color spectrum. The primary and other colors in an additive process such as video are those of the light itself. Combined, the primary colors create white light.

⇒ Film uses a subtractive color process in which complementary colors—yellow, magenta, and cyan—create the rest of the color spectrum. Subtractive color processes are based on the interaction of substances with white light. The color dyes on film, for example, absorb specific colors or color ranges from the white light passing through them and allow only a desired color light to be projected. See also *subtractive color system*.

address track time code

☐ The time code that is recorded at a different frequency but in the same physical location as the picture on three-quarter-inch and all half-inch professional video recordings. Address track time code is not related to the tape's control track. See also *control track*.

⇒ Kodak's Keykode™ symbols are written in bar code along the edge of film. It takes a special machine to decode Keykode. The Keykode system also includes human readable code imprint on the film. The standard means of identifying film frames and footage is either by latent edge numbers from the film negative or by separate code printed on the film edge during the post-production process.

ADO™

☐ Brand name of a digital video effects device; represents the manufacturer's name: Ampex Digital Optics. The digital video effects (DVE) device allows certain types of manipulation of the video frame. (Although many people in the video industry use ADO as a generic term for any digital video effects device, ADO is a particular DVE generator.) The effects device creates effects but does not generate the image within the effect.

Typically available DVE moves are zoom in or out, from or to anywhere in the video raster; mirror imaging (flips); repositioning of the video rectangle; and zooming past normal size.

⇒ The optical printer is the DVE of film. Film effects would include egg boxes, gutters, and many different types of traveling mattes. Other equivalents would be flips and flop-overs. See also *digital video effects (DVE)*; *effects*.

 ADR See *Automatic Dialogue Replacement*.

advance

📹 The number of frames on a composite film (a film that includes picture and audio) between the picture frame and its synchronized sound. This separation compensates for a significant distance within a projection device between the film gate and the audio playback heads.

➥ Even though every videotape machine has an offset between the audio and picture heads, in practical operation, this advance is essentially negligible and not readily seen.

☐ **AFT** See *automatic fine tuning.*

⚡ **AGC** See *automatic gain control.*

air copy
☐ A final version of a video released for broadcast transmission.
➥ The film analogy would be the release print, a copy intended for distribution.

⚡ **albedo** The ratio of incident light to reflected light; the fraction of the light hitting a surface that the surface will reflect back.

☐ **aliasing** The jagged edges seen in diagonal or circular lines within a video picture caused by the fact that the television signal is created by straight horizontal-scan lines. This effect is somewhat lessened in newer character generators and other effects devices. The term for eliminating aliasing in a video device is *anti-aliasing.*

☐ **alignment tape** A test tape, with video and audio signals on it, made by the manufacturer for the purpose of adjusting record and playback functions.

⚡ **ambient sound** Natural background audio heard on a location or in a studio, without dialogue or other production-created sound. Every area in the world has its own unique ambient sound created by machinery, weather, or animate objects. These sounds change over time (as a plane takes off, as traffic increases or decreases, as an animal passes, etc.).

Most sound recordists record several minutes of ambient sound during production at each location to aid the sound editor in cutting. In film production, this is sometimes called an *atmos* (atmosphere) *loop.* With ambient sound, the editor can fill spaces between dialogue or effects with the sound from that exact area, thus creating a seamless audio track. See also *room tone.*

☐ **Ampex** A United States-based video company credited with the discovery and development of videotape recording. It remains a powerful manufacturing and development firm, bringing the ADO™ and VPR™ videotape machines, the ZEUS™ time-base corrector, and other developments to the video production and post-production scene.

⚡ **amplitude** The scientific measure of the comparative intensity of a signal. Most commonly used to measure the loudness of sound, not to be confused with the subjective judgment of sound called *loudness.* Amplitude is measured in decibels. See also *decibel; volume unit; VU meter.*

⚡ **analog** Electronic signals (audio or video) that are sent, received, and stored in the form of varying voltages continuously proportional to the original signal. Analog signals degrade with each copy or generation. In contrast, digital signals degrade very little with each generation. Each copy is extremely close to, if not equal to, the quality of the original recording. See also *digital video*.

Most film equipment is analog. However, there are new film devices, like digital audio and digital film devices, that are being used in film production and post-production processes. Most video formats are analog with the exception of the D1, D2, and D3 machines. Most audio recordings are analog, but digital audio tape (DAT), compact disks (CDs), and digital audio workstations (DAWs) use digital encoding and are being used in visual industry. See also *digital*.

anamorphic lens   A lens that compresses the horizontal width of a wide-screen format image into a standard-size film gauge. Upon projection, another anamorphic lens expands the image into a wide-screen format.

animate   To photograph still images or objects with the purpose of giving them the appearance of movement when the film or tape is replayed. Film animation is done with cells and pin-registered artwork. Video animation is usually accomplished through the use of a graphics or paint system.

answer print

The first print(s) of a completed film project that come from the film laboratory, with opticals and audio track included. These are the prints that will be submitted for approval before the process of manufacturing release prints is begun. Color and density of the picture and the quality of the optical sound reproduction are the primary concerns in the answer print.

It often takes several attempts to produce a totally acceptable answer print of a film.

The equivalent of an answer print would be the *sweetened edited master*. An edited master, created during the on-line session, includes the final picture and opticals. A sweetened edited master contains the final picture along with the final mixed audio track(s). All duplication of the program would originate from an approved sweetened edited master. See also *on-line; sweetening*.

antihalation backing   See *back coating*.

aperture   The opening in a camera that alters the amount of light that reaches the film, pickup tube, or CCD.

aperture mask   Also known as a **shadow mask**. Both a widely used color video monitor technology and a specific component device.

The mask is a perforated, screenlike material positioned just behind the faceplate within a cathode ray tube. The faceplate is covered with an array of red, green, and blue phosphor dots that illuminate when struck by any combination of red, green, and blue electron beams projected from the tube's opposite end. The perforations of the aperture mask precisely coordinate the electron beams, thus ensuring that the mosaic of phosphors are properly excited to create an accurate viewing image.

arc

A curved camera move.

A light that provides high-intensity light through the use of an electron current that passes from one electrode to another. This type of light is being replaced by HMIs. See also *lighting*.

Arriflex™   Brand name of a high-quality film camera that brought 16-millimeter into professional acceptance. The Arriflex company also manufactures high quality 35-millimeter cameras for professional use.

art card   A piece of paper or cardboard onto which is printed or drawn artwork for reproduction. In film, the art card is shot by a camera and can be combined with a picture through the use of an optical printer. In video, the art card is shot with a video camera, recorded onto videotape, and then loaded into a video paint system or character generator. Effects may or may not be included during the process. See also *effects (video)*; *opticals*.

ASA (American Standard Association) exposure index

The ASA number on a film designates the film's relative sensitivity to light. The ASA scale is an arithmetic scale. A film with an ASA of 100 would be half as sensitive as a film with an ASA rating of 200, and, thus, the former would require twice as much light as the latter.

Film with a lower ASA number has smaller halides closer together and produces a sharper, fine-grained picture; it also requires more light for exposure. Film with an ASA number below 75 is considered to be lower-speed film. Medium-speed film is ASA 75–125. Film with an ASA number of 126 to 150 is considered normal and higher than 150 is considered fast.

DIN is an alternative, logarithmic exposure index in which each progression of three degrees represents a doubling of film photosensitivity. Table 1 is a comparison of the ASA index to the DIN index.

The stock used in videotape does not determine the light levels required for an image recording. It is the camera's pickup tube or its charge coupled device (CCD) that determines the light sensitivity. This is most often expressed in the number of foot candles required to create a picture. See also *foot candle*.

There are different quality levels of videotape stocks that have progressively fewer dropouts, better reception, and better retention of electrical signals. Metal tape is more sensitive and of a higher quality but costs more and should be used with a compatible tape machine. Broadcast-quality tape has fewer dropouts than consumer videotape. See also *dropout*.

Table 1. ASA–DIN Conversion Table

ASA	DIN	ASA	DIN
50	18	200	24
64	19	250	25
80	20	320	26
100	21	400	27
125	22	500	28
160	23	650	29

aspect ratio

 Screen size as expressed by the ratio of the width to the height. The aspect ratio of a picture is dependent on the stock used, the production format, and the releasing medium. There are more available aspect ratios to choose from in film than in video. Video is limited by having basically only two commercially acceptable ratios, only one of which is found in the United States.

 The standard, or academy, aspect ratio is 1.33:1 (ironically the same ratio as the standard television projection in the United States). There are various other formats available (Figure 8). The most commonly used aspect ratios are 1.66:1, 1.76:1, and 1.85:1, all wide-screen formats. Some movies are shot on the standard 1.33:1 format, then blown up and cropped. This results in a wider picture, but the image is slightly inferior to the original 1.33:1 footage.

Super 16 has the same aspect ratio as 35-millimeter film and can be blown up to any 35-millimeter aspect ratio. Two other standards are Vista Vision, with a 2.21:1 ratio, and Super Vision (or Super Panavision), with a 2.4:1 ratio. Vista Vision shoots scenes sideways on the film.

Television format has a 4:3 aspect ratio, which is the same as the Academy ratio (1.33:1). The only other commercial format that might be considered is the existing Japanese High Definition format, called Hi-Vision, which is in a 1.78:1 ratio. There most likely will be one or two more wide-screen video formats developed and commercially available in the next several years. Both Europe and the United States are going to formally adopt high-definition formats in the very near future.

If a program is produced on film in a format wider than the Academy standard and transferred to videotape, some portion of the picture has to be cropped or eliminated. The active choosing of the portion of the picture that is to be seen is called *panning and scanning*.

An alternative to panning and scanning the film is to transfer the total width of the motion picture to videotape and have a black mask at the top and bottom of the screen. This method of transferring is called a *letter box* and is often used for title sequences of feature films because

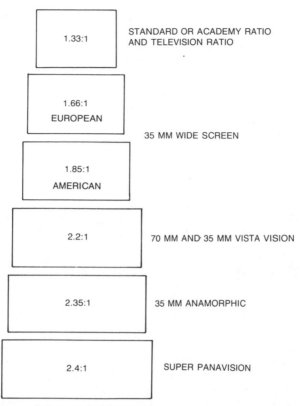

Figure 8 Several standard format projection aspect ratios. Note that the smallest 35-millimeter format, Academy, is the same as that of television.

panning and scanning might eliminate names or cut off portions of titles. The letter box is occasionally seen in music videos, where it is an accepted form of broadcasting.

assemble edit

- The assemble edit is a production or scene that includes all component shots, with their slates, or heads, and tails, assembled in proper viewing order. The *fine cut* is created by eliminating the slate, tail, and other unneeded footage from the assemble edit. See also *rough cut*.

- The video equivalent generally would be the product of an off-line editing session during which preliminary decisions about shot selections are made, based upon window dubs (copies) of the originally recorded material. The resulting video can then be viewed and refined before a more selective off-line process begins that produces the final video master.

☐ **1.** The stringing together of *completed* programs or self-contained segments. Commercial or demo reels are often created by successively copying individual elements onto one reel. This routine editing procedure is often called an assemble edit, as there is no demanding creativity needed to piece completed programs together, back to back. It is not unusual to use assemble recordings during an assemble edit session.

2. The automated process of on-line editing. Many producers use the words *assemble edit session* to indicate an on-line editing session. In the early days of video on-line editing, an electronic edit that held up to repeated playback was a marvelous achievement. At that time, video editing merely consisted of stringing completed segments together—an assembly of video.

Since those pioneer days, video post-production has become immensely more sophisticated, but the misnomer of an assemble edit session for what really is an on-line editing session is still used occasionally. See also *auto-assembly*.

➡ An answer print is the final version of a film submitted for approval before release prints are made.

assemble recording

☐ The technical method of recording audio, video, and control track onto videotape. Assemble recordings replace every signal on the videotape, most importantly the control track, as this ensures a constant speed reference throughout the tape's length. Blank videotapes for editing purposes often are prepared by assemble recording time code, control track, and, for the video, black over their length.

Insert recording, in which only the video and/or audio components are recorded or replaced, is only performed on tape that has been assemble recorded and, thus, has control-track pulses.

Most professional dubbing, or copying of videotape, is performed using assemble recordings. Most professional editing is performed using insert recordings.

➡ A physical film equivalent to an assemble recording would be the cutting of sprocket holes into a film stock during the manufacturing process. Sprocket holes, like control-track pulses on videotape, act as a guide for playback at a consistent speed.

atmos loop See *ambient sound*.

ATR See *audio tape recorder*.

audio tape recorder (ATR) A machine that receives inputted audio signals from a microphone or other source and records them onto magnetic tape, often with the ability to be used by remote control and with the capability to record multiple tracks.

auto-assembly

☐ The automatic editing of a video program during an on-line editing session. Given an edit decision list (EDL), a video program can be automatically conformed (constructed from its component takes) by an on-line computer. Certain parameters must be adhered to for a successful auto-assembly. The EDL must be perfect, with no overlapping edits. Also, all the necessary playback reels must be available in the editing house.

Auto-assemblies are often used for sitcoms, commercials, and episodic shows. Most of these are situations where the video recording conditions were under total control. For instance, a sitcom is usually shot in a television studio where the video cameras are all perfectly balanced. The lighting in a studio is under the careful scrutiny of a lighting director who has the use of a grid, series of dimmers, and a stationary set, all of which result in a similar look from each camera.

In the case of commercials, most are shot on film and then transferred to videotape via a telecine. In the transferring process, the film is color corrected and positioned for viewing by the telecine operator (colorist). By the time the on-line editor receives the footage, it is ready to be cut together quickly, so an auto-assembly is a perfectly logical choice. See also *telecine*.

An auto-assembly is usually not performed when the footage is from the field, such as in a documentary. Each shot might need to be color balanced relative to the previous shot. An auto-assembly would not be appropriate for a movie commercial either. The feature film might be telecined and color timed, but, because of the juxtaposition of shots from different areas in the film, its color might require fine tuning.

If a computerized list is not available, an auto-assembly cannot be performed. Also, often video effects are created during the on-line editing session. This does not allow for an auto-assembly as the effects need to be created and approved during the editing session. Some producers choose to on-line edit their effects before the auto-assembly and include the prebuilt effect in the computerized EDL. See also *mode*.

To conclude, an auto-assembly is performed when all the technical elements of the program have been dealt with, and all that remains is a perfunctory assembly of the show's elements with minimal effects (dissolves, wipes, and keys).

⇒ The auto-assembly is like the lab processing an answer print. All the opticals have been performed, the negative cutter has conformed all the camera's original footage, the negative has been timed, and all that remains is the lab's job of running the footage through the lab.

automatic dialogue replacement (ADR)   Also called **looping**. A process that replaces production audio with audio from a sound studio. This post-production technique is accomplished by replaying the scene over and over in the sound studio while the performer lip-syncs to the picture. There are various reasons for replacing production audio, which might include uncontrollable set sound sources like planes, weather, cars, or loud background sounds. Another reason for ADR might be that a director is unsatisfied with a performer's original read or wants to change a line.

The ADR process requires a playback source, which can be a film loop or computer-programmed videotape, and some type of audio recording device. The new audio can be recorded onto any of the following formats: film mag, quarter-inch audiotape, videotape, or multitrack.

During the ADR session, the scene is played back repeatedly until the ADR editor and/or director is satisfied that the performer has read the line correctly. Then the audio is sent onto the dialogue editor to be placed into the program.

automatic fine tuning (AFT)   An electronic device found in certain television sets that adjusts the set's signal receiver for the best possible reception. A sensor in the set adjusts the tuning of the set's channel selector to the strongest signal strength.

automatic gain control (AGC)   An electronic circuit that adjusts for variations in incoming audio or video levels, maintaining the output at some preset level or range of levels. In an audio circuit, a weaker input signal can be amplified automatically to a consistent higher level. A fluctuating level can be rendered constant. In a video circuit, the brighter the source, the smaller the aperture opening. As a rule, these types of circuits are not used in professional production since the cinematographer and audio recordist usually want control of all elements of the recording.

In some video productions, especially in news location shooting, AGC *video* circuits are employed, but AGCs in audio situations usually fluctuate too much to be acceptable. Both audio and video AGCs are used extensively in home video camcorders of all formats. See also *gain control.*

B negative

🎥 The negative of all the takes of a film that the director has not requested for printing. This footage is developed and filed. Occasionally, this footage is retrieved and used for editing.

📺 Since video processing is an electronic transfer process, original footage, either needed or rejected, is not physically separated, and, thus, both selected and rejected footage will be located on the same reel of original tape. Unless the whole reel is determined to be unnecessary, production footage is kept available until the show is completed.

B reel See *B roll*.

B roll

🎥 The incoming shot of an A/B roll.

📺 **1.** A copy of an original tape (a dub) made in order to create an effect when both shots required for the final shot are on the same reel.

 2. Background or extra material shot for cutaways in a news or information playback reel.

B scene

🎥 The right side of two pieces of film about to be cut together. Basically the scene being cut to.

📺 The incoming scene or shot.

B – Y (B minus Y)

📺 The color-difference signal that is the result of the subtraction of the luminance signal (Y) from the blue signal (B). The Y signal is recombined with B to produce primary blue. See also *component video*.

📺 The film equivalent is the blue-sensitive emulsion; the area of film that is sensitive to the blue-colored aspect of the image.

🎥 **back coating** Also called **backing** and **antihalation backing**. A material placed on the outside of the film base to prevent light that has passed through the various layers of emulsion from bouncing back and

13

creating a halo effect. The backcoating is washed off during the film's processing.

back focus

☐ A physical adjustment to the electronic device that converts light to electronic pulses. This adjustment alters the distance between the rear element of the lens and the face of the pickup device (CCD or camera tube, for example).

⇐ The film equivalent would be to move the film plane in order to adjust the camera's focus. Note that film cameras generally are focused by moving the lens relative to the film plane and not the other way around.

back lot   A location for a production shoot that is outdoors but still at a studio's facility.

back porch   That part of the television signal between the tail edge of horizontal sync and the tail edge of corresponding blanking. See also *blanking*.

background

1. The area farthest away from the camera in a shot. See also *foreground*.
2. The history of a character before the start of the story to be filmed or taped.
3. In an effect, the part of the image that appears to be farthest from the audience.

backing

The financial source of any project as well as the strength of that source.

See *back coating*.

backtime   The timing of a scene so that a specific part of the scene occurs at a specified moment. Backtiming is used in production to coordinate two or more actions occurring at the same time. In post-production, backtiming is a common process. Because the action is locked to a definite duration, the editor can calculate an edit so that a certain action occurs at a certain music beat or narration or dialogue word. Audio can be backtimed to coincide with picture as well.

balance stripe

A stripe of magnetic material placed along the side of the film opposite the side with the magnetic sound track to ensure that the film is the same thickness on both sides in order to keep the film from rewinding unevenly.

⇐ When plastic one-inch tapes are used on certain one-inch-tape video machines, a metal reel is placed on the supply reel to balance it with the metal takeup reel in order to keep the tension between the two reels balanced.

banner

Short pieces of film used during post-production to indicate placement of currently missing or forthcoming segments. The banner is edited into the film as an identifier until the proper material is available. Specific information about the missing film is normally printed onto the banner. This might include why the film is outstanding (*scene missing*) or the type of material that will occupy the space (*commercial, freeze frame* or other types of optical effects, and so on). By using banners as placeholders, the production staff can do a preliminary assessment of the overall flow of the film without waiting for all of the material.

In video, the term *slug* is used, rather than *banner*, although the purpose of the item is basically the same. The identifying information normally would be created with a character generator. Occasionally a film banner is transferred to videotape for use in tape editing.

bars See *color bars*.

base A tough, transparent, flexible material onto which the emulsion is fixed (Figure 9). Film base is usually cellulose triacetate. In the early days of film, nitrate was used as a base. Nitrate, however, is extremely flammable and extremely dangerous.

The base for videotape is usually Mylar, a trade name for polyethylene terephthalate, a plastic that was developed in the early days of the space program. Film base is thicker than the videotape base.

bath

The processing solution for film, usually in a developer or its container tanks. The film is totally immersed in a large body of developing fluid in order to chemically treat the emulsion, developing and fixing the photographic image (Figure 10).

A parallel comparison would be the video head that writes the picture information to the videotape. As the bath helps the image to be stored on the film, so does the video head help the image to be stored.

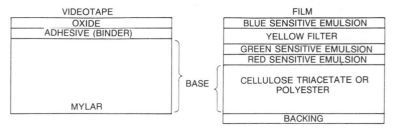

Figure 9 Film and video base. Both film and videotape have a similar construction: a strong base and a softer recording medium bonded to it.

Figure 10   Developer. A black-and-white developer. Film is run deep into each compartment, then looped over a roller to enter the next bath. Photo by Sean Sterling, courtesy of Cinema Research Corporation.

bay
   Where scenery is stored.
   A part of a facility where specific work takes place, for example, a telecine bay, an editing bay (Figure 11).
   The word *room* or *stage* replaces *bay* in the film lexicon—editing room, projection room, viewing room, sound stage, ADR stage, dubbing stage.

bayonet mount   A type of fitting for camera lenses that requires a push and then a twist to lock the lens to the body of the camera. See also *c mount*.

beam splitter   A glass block that diverts a portion of light to a viewfinder, video assist, or light meter, allowing the rest of the light to pass. Neither the diverted light nor the primary beam are degraded or substantially altered by this process. Beam splitters can be found in telecine electronics, film cameras, film chains, and so on.

bellows   A folding sleeve that is inserted between the body of the camera and the lens to increase the distance between the lens and the film plane; most often used for close up work.

bells on (bells off)   On a set or sound stage, an audio and visual signal that indicates that a recording session is in progress and absolute quiet is called for. *Bells off* indicates that the recording session is over.

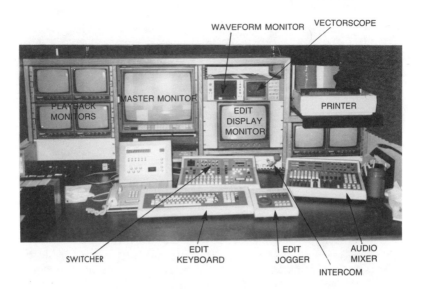

Figure 11   Video editing bay. This small editing bay contains many of the common elements, including the often-used phone. Photo by Sean Sterling, courtesy of Video Research Corporation.

below the line   Financial term for costs of the technical crew and other production costs (camera, stock, camera crew, and so on). As a general rule, below-the-line costs are fixed costs, those that can be budgeted accurately per hour of production. See also *above the line*.

Betacam™   Trade name of a professional half-inch video format created by the Sony Corporation that records luminance separately from the chrominance, has address track capability, and two channels of audio. Betacam is compatible with Betacam SP, the next generation of Sony's half-inch format, which has a longer recording capability and four channels of audio. Competitors of this brand name format would be Panasonic's MII and one-inch videotape formats. See also *component video signal*. Betacam has been a standard format in news and low- to medium-budget video productions.

⟺ Betacam is an accepted, standard, broadcast- (distribution-) quality video format. As such, it has the same regard within the video community as 35-millimeter film does within the film community. See also *formats*.

Betamax™

The Sony Corporation's home-video format that competes with their own more recently developed 8-millimeter format Hi-8 and Panasonic's popular VHS format. The Betamax tape is one-half inch wide.

⟺ This format placed in its video hierarchy would be the equivalent of 8-millimeter or super 8 film. See also *formats*.

binder

☐ Material used to adhere magnetic particles of videotape stock to each other as well as to the base material.

⇐ The film equivalent to videotape's binder is a subcoat that adheres the three photosensitive emulsion layers and a yellow filter layer to the support or base of the film.

bins

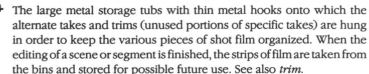

The large metal storage tubs with thin metal hooks onto which the alternate takes and trims (unused portions of specific takes) are hung in order to keep the various pieces of shot film organized. When the editing of a scene or segment is finished, the strips of film are taken from the bins and stored for possible future use. See also *trim*.

⇐ There are two video equivalents to the film editor's bins. The first is a large metal cart with casters on the bottom. Since videotape editing does not require that the tape be physically cut, there are no trims as in film. However, each tape occupies space and carts are used to store the tapes for editing sessions and to transport tapes within a building. When an editing session is completed, tapes usually are removed from the cart and either returned to the client or stored in a vault.

The second video *bin* is electronic. Many of the more advanced video-editing systems have electronic storage areas, called *bins*, that hold one or more edit decision lists. Some random-access editing systems use bins to hold electronic pictures for use during the editing session.

bipack

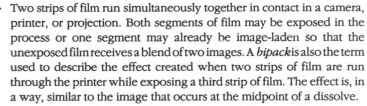

Two strips of film run simultaneously together in contact in a camera, printer, or projection. Both segments of film may be exposed in the process or one segment may already be image-laden so that the unexposed film receives a blend of two images. A *bipack* is also the term used to describe the effect created when two strips of film are run through the printer while exposing a third strip of film. The effect is, in a way, similar to the image that occurs at the midpoint of a dissolve.

⇐ The video equivalent of the bipack would be a modified mix or nonadditive mix. In both cases, the two images are combined in a dissolve, but to create the effect of a bipack, rather than completing the dissolve, the midpoint of the effect is held for some specified amount of time. Some production switchers (such as the Grass Valley 300) have a transition called a nonadditive mix, which is not commonly used. This effect is a special type of dissolve bringing in the white values of the incoming shot first while fading out the white values of the outgoing shot last. At the midpoint of the effect, rather than having each shot at a 50 percent overall value, the white levels of the two shots are much brighter than in a normal dissolve.

black level

☐ The amplitude of the signal representing the darkest part of a video image as measured on a videoscope. In the United States' broadcast standard, the lowest allowable exposure of video that can be *broadcast* is called the *pedestal*. This amount of black is measured at 7.5 percent of white level above the blanking level. In the United States' broadcast format as defined by the Federal Communications Commission, picture information is not supposed to fall below this level of black.

In post-production effects creation, this level is often exceeded and can be as low as −6 percent, allowing for more latitude in creating effects. See also *blanking*.

The film equivalent would be the toe of film's characteristic curve. Although the characteristic curve is a physical limitation of a film stock's sensitivity to light, it still indicates the top and bottom of the film's light-sensitivity range, whereas the black-and-white level of the waveform indicates the video signal's strengths, not its electronic limitations.

blanking

A periodic and regular signal within a video signal that prevents video information from appearing on the face of a cathode ray tube or video monitor, allowing the scanning beam to strategically reposition itself horizontally or vertically. As the scanning beam of a picture tube travels from one end of the line of picture information to the beginning of the next, it cannot make any visible signal marks on the face of the tube. The blanking signal blacks out the video information while the beam is repositioned; the duration of the blackout is called the horizontal blanking interval, or period. Included in the horizontal blanking period are the front porch, back porch, horizontal sync, and color reference burst.

Similarly, as the scanning beam resets from the lower right corner of a completed video field to the top left of a new field, a blanking signal blacks out the video information. This duration is called the vertical blanking interval, or period. Included in the vertical blanking period are synchronizing pulses, the ability to record test patterns, time code, and closed-captioning information. See also *field; scanning*.

Blanking can be compared to the horizontal frame lines and vertical frame borders in film. Given that the vertical blanking defines sequential units of picture information, it is analogous to the frame lines that physically separate film frames. Note, however, that in the United States' video standard, a full frame of picture information consists of two interwoven half-frames, or fields, and, thus, vertical blanking occurs twice for each complete video frame.

Similarly, the horizontal blanking, by suppressing the electron beam within a CRT, defines by its timing the width of the video image. In this sense, it is analogous to the edges of the film frame defined by the film format and the camera aperture or gate.

blanking interval   See *blanking period.*

blanking level   A reference point, in a composite video signal, corresponding with zero signal level. Below this level, there are sync pulses; above this level, in the positive direction, picture signals appear. See also *black level; blanking; composite video signal; sync.*

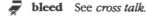 **blanking period** Also called the **blanking interval.** The time that the video scanning beam in a picture tube is blacked out as it moves from the end of one line to the beginning of another or from the end of one video field to the next.

bleed See *cross talk.*

blinking
- Turning on and off a title or object on the screen. This is accomplished through the use of prepared film elements combined in an optical printer. See also *effects.*
- The video equivalent is *flashing.* Usually this effect is created by either a character generator (when titles are involved) or by the manipulation of the video switcher.

blocking The rehearsal concentrating on the physical placement and movement of actors and equipment; also, the physical positioning of on-screen elements thus determined.

bloom
- Excessive light glare, often resulting in a halo around a light area. Basically, this effect occurs because the halides are so overexposed by the excessive light that the neighboring particles are also affected, even though they were not themselves overexposed.
- The video equivalent would be *tearing.* Video tearing is caused by excessive light or color (chroma) transmitted to the videotape.

blow up To enlarge a picture or a section of a picture.

blowup An enlargement of a picture or graphic. See *opticals.*

blue backing
- The physical background used in production for blue-screen effects. See also *blue-screen effect.*
- In video production, this backing is called a chroma key blue, just as the electronic effect is often called a chroma key. See also *chroma key.*

blue-screen effect
- An effect in which a character or object is photographed in front of a blue backing or screen. Later, in an optical printer, that object or character is combined with a background image by eliminating the blue area of the foreground. This process is used in conjunction with a variety of special effects, including but not limited to miniature photography, flying effects, outer space shots, and so on.
- The video equivalent would be a chroma key effect. This electronic effect is accomplished in a way very similar to film by using a colored (usually blue) background and then electronically eliminating that color and inserting another picture. See also *chroma key.*

boom   An extendible, often polelike, support mount for audio or camera equipment that enables such equipment to be positioned in otherwise difficult-to-reach places. For example, a microphone can be placed immediately above the actors, capturing quality sound without interfering with the shot; a camera can be placed for high-angle shots and can move smoothly from a high- to a low-angle shot, and vice versa. A boom can be very simple or very complicated and expensive; a boom may also be a part of a camera itself, supporting heavy optional components such as zoom lenses.

booth   An observation, screening, or recording room (as in audio booth, control booth, etc.).

break down   Separating dailies into individual takes on their own separate reels and syncing audio with the picture.

breakdown   The pre-production detail of shooting schedule and necessary production resources.

breakup
☐ An interrupted signal or picture image distortion.
⇐ The film equivalent would be an interruption during the filming or projection process causing a distorted picture.

☐ **breezeway**   The portion of the back porch between the trailing edge of the sync pulse and the start of color burst. See also *blanking.*

bridge
An musical segment designed to help the transition from one location or time to another.
☐ An overhead rack or permanent mount for equipment.

brightness range   Ratio between darkest and lightest portions of a picture. See also *characteristic curve; contrast.*

budget   The amount of financial expenditures expected or allowed to be used for a portion of a project or the entire completed production. See also *above the line, below the line.*

bulk erase
☐ Also known as **degauss.** To remove at one time *all* previously recorded signal information, including control track, on a reel of videotape or audiotape. This is done by placing the tape close to a very strong magnetic source, such as a bulk eraser. See also *bulk eraser.*
⇐ Film cannot be unexposed; however, it can be recycled.

☐ **bulk eraser**   A device that creates an extremely strong magnetic field that destroys previously recorded signals on video- and audio-tape. The bulk eraser demagnetizes the tape and is capable of also affecting checks, credit cards, and any other magnetic device. See also *bulk erase.*

☐ **burn-in**   Temporary or permanent damage to a camera tube caused by focusing it on an excessively strong light source.

☐ **butt cut**   See *butt edit.*

☐ **butt edit**   Also known as **butt cut**. To immediately cut to the next shot.

🎥 **butt splice**   See *tape splice.*

🎥 **butt splicer**   See *splicer.*

buzz track

🎥 1. A test film with a special optical sound recorded on it for the purpose of determining the correct position of the scanning slit of an optical sound recorder.

↪ The video equivalent would be an *alignment tape.*

2. Natural-set or location sound recorded on a track and used as a background source for mixing behind dialogue or narration. See also *ambient sound* and *room tone.*

↪ A *room tone loop* or a *slug of ambient sound* would be the video equivalent.

c mount A camera lens mount that uses a one-inch outer-diameter thread and 12 threads to the inch; a screw-in/screw-out type of mount.

call sheet A daily schedule showing production details and schedules. Information usually includes where and when the production takes place and who is to be where and at what time.

camera

A machine that directs light onto a recording medium, while also allowing an operator to view the image that is being transferred (Figure 12).

A film camera exposes a piece of a strip of film to light for a specific amount of time, then moves the film an exact amount so that the next portion of the film can be exposed. The film camera also allows a human operator to view the image that is being recorded on the film.

An additional objective of the camera might include sending the viewed image onto another device (additional monitors or a video-assist system).

A video camera directs light onto an electronic device (CCD or tube) that converts the light into an electronic signal, then sends that signal out of the camera through the use of wire(s).

The video camera also allows a human operator to view, through a device called a viewfinder, exactly the image that is being recorded on the tape.

camera angle The general camera position in relationship to the action (often found in scripts), as well as the distance the camera is from the action. In actual use, the camera angle is often spelled out, while the distance from the action is most often abbreviated.

Distance:

LS —Long shot CU — Close-up
WS — Wide shot ECU — Extreme close-up
MS — Medium shot

THE CAMERAS

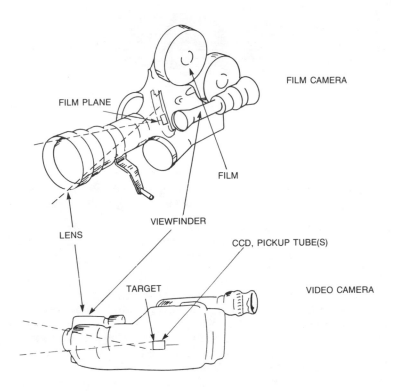

FILM CAMERA

FILM PLANE

FILM

VIEWFINDER

LENS

CCD, PICKUP TUBE(S)

TARGET   VIDEO CAMERA

Figure 12   The camera. Both film and video cameras have a similar purpose: to expose a recording system to a select amount of focused light.

Angle:
Low angle — the camera is placed low, on the ground or floor.
High angle — the camera is located above the action, often on a crane.
Straight on — the camera is located directly facing the action. In a close-up, it would be at eye level. In a wider shot, it would probably be slightly lower than eye level.

camera assistant
An individual assigned to help in preparing, loading, and shooting with the camera. This person performs functions critical to the operation of the camera.

The video equivalent would be a videotape operator, the individual responsible for preparing, loading, and monitoring the videotape recorder.

☐ **camera cue light** Also called **tally light**. Located on top of an electronic camera, a light (often red) that indicates which particular camera of several in a multicamera production is recording or on the air.

camera matching

☐ The process of coordinating the controls and technical settings of different cameras so that the pictures from the different cameras look the same.

➡ Although the comparison is not a direct one, making sure the same film stock and exposure factor is used throughout a scene or during multicamera shooting would be a similar situation as camera matching.

camera operator

📷 The person who operates the film camera during production. Responsibilities also include checking the camera's gate after each shot, monitoring the shot during the action, and looking for and logging any camera problems (for example, audio boom in the shot, unintended intrusions in the background, focus errors, unwanted camera movement, etc.).

➡ In single-camera video production, the camera operator is responsible for loading the camera and watching for visual problems. In studio work, the camera feed is usually sent to a control booth where the director and/or technical director also watch for technical problems.

📼 **camera original** The film or videotape that comes directly from the camera. The physical camera original, the first exposed or recorded element of a shot, can be videotape, film negative, or film positive.

camera report

📷 Forms filled out by an assistant camera person listing takes and indicating specifically which takes to print, as well as problems, comments, directives, weather conditions, and/or other applicable remarks that concern the film-processing lab. See also *logs*.

➡ The video equivalent is the production assistant's script notes, taken during production. Another comparison would be the master log, a record of all production footage made after production, during a logging session.

📼 **camera support** Any device upon which a camera rests. These devices would include: a tripod, camera clamp, dolly, crane, body brace, image stabilizer, Steadicam™.

cans

📼 A casual name for earphones.

📷 Metal containers used for film storage.

capstan

☐ A rotating spindle used to move tape through a machine. Capstans are found in video as well as audio machines.

⇐ The pulldown claw is the mechanism that moves the film through the camera's gate. Pulldown claws are used in film projectors as well as film cameras.

capstan servo

☐ An electronically controlled motor that drives the capstan, which in turn moves the tape through the machine. This device maintains control of tape speed during record or playback.

⇐ The crystal-controlled motor inside a film camera maintains accurate control of the film mechanism speed.

cardioid microphone   A unidirectional microphone that has a pickup pattern in the shape of a heart. See also *omnidirectional microphone; shotgun microphone.*

cart machine   A computer-controlled videotape player that holds numerous short videotape cartridges. The cartridges are loaded into a tractorlike mechanism that moves the tapes into position for playback. Usually found in larger television stations and networks, these machines are loaded with several hours worth of commercials that are automatically played at predetermined times.

cathode ray

☐ Part of the image-scanning process, the stream of electrons emitted by an electron gun within a vacuum tube; the gun scans the phosphor-coated inner surface of the tube, creating an illuminated video image. See also *blanking; scanning.*

⇐ A film analogy would be the light emitted from a film projector's lamp and the image-laden light emitted by the projector itself before it is realized upon a screen.

cathode ray tube (CRT)

☐ The electronic device, a type of vacuum tube, that creates the picture in a television set by sending a directed stream of electrons at a phosphorous material that covers the inner viewing surface of the tube. Cathode ray tubes also are the picture-creating elements found in computer monitors, vectorscopes, and oscilloscopes. See also *scanning.*

⇐ A film analogy would be a combination of the projector and the room where a film is projected. The image information passes from the projector through the room and is directed at a screen.

CCD   See *charge coupled device.*

CDS   See *cinema digital sound.*

CdS meter   Also called **exposure meter**. A device that measures the amount of light reflected from a subject and uses a cadmium sulfide cell as its light sensor. Reflected light can be very different than the light falling on a subject. It is the reflected light that is recorded on film.

cement splice   The joining together of two separate pieces of film by use of cement. A specially designed blade on a device called a cement splicer is used to scrape a portion of the emulsion off one piece of film. Then cement is placed on the scraped area. Then the second piece of film is attached to the first through the use of the splicer causing a small, unnoticeable overlap. A heating element in the splicer speeds the curing of the cement. Cement splices are used almost exclusively in negative cutting as the splice is extremely strong and permanent. See also *splicer.*

 cement splicer   See *splicer.*

 change over cue   A dot, circle, or other signal near the end of a film or video reel that warns an operator or projectionist that it is time to change reels. Changeover cues in the theater can be seen at the top right hand of the movie picture, usually every 15 to 20 minutes in 35-millimeter film. There are also aural signals on projectors that warn the projectionist that the reel needs to be changed.

In the past, changeover cues were also used in television for feature-film broadcasts. However, since most feature films are now aired from videotape with longer playback times, rather than 16-millimeter dupes, the television need for changeover cues has diminished.

 changing bag   A light-tight bag used to handle film without danger of exposing the film to light.

character generator

☐ An electronic device that creates letters and symbols in video (Figure 13). Various character generators have different abilities. Top-of-the-line character generators can perform complicated animation and other effects. In addition, most high-end character generators can send a hi-con or external key cuts to the video switcher, allowing users to cut an exact hole out of the background picture. Examples of these devices can be seen on network sports programs.

The least expensive character generators can only type poorly formed alpha-numeric characters and are used only for video identification.

⇒ The film equivalent would be the developed film of a graphics card, a simple, text-only art card. In the case of high-end, animation-capable character generators, the comparison would be title or animation footage composited in an optical printer as well as the corresponding hi-con footage.

characteristic curve

 A graph that expresses the exposure attributes of a particular film stock, specifically the logarithmic relation between the intensity of exposure to light and the density of the resulting image on the recording medium (Figure 14).

Figure 13 The keyboard and video displays of a character generator. The actual working parts of the machine are usually in another room mounted in an equipment rack. Photo by Sean Sterling, courtesy of Video Research Corporation.

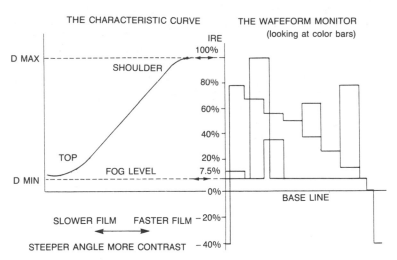

Figure 14 Film's characteristic curve and video waveform monitors have similar aspects. The characteristic curve is already a physical reality for a particular film stock. The waveform indicates possibilities of video recording and playback. Where exposure cannot fall below the fog level of a film stock, video recordings can fall below broadcast's technical limit of 7.5 percent. The upper limits are similar on the two graphs. Overexposure is bright white, on either mediums.

The graph is created by exposing a test strip of film to increasing amounts of light, developing the film, and, finally, charting the results of the test.

The characteristic curve of a particular film stock indicates the contrast sensitivity, exposure latitude, and the light sensitivity of the film stock. Contrast sensitivity compares, for a particular type of film, the relative distinctness of darkest and lightest portions of the picture and the accompanying definition of midcolor ranges. Exposure latitude is simply the range of light intensity that will have any effect at all on a particular type of film, the boundaries being the darkness too dark for the film to record and the brightness that whites out any other images. A high-contrast film will have a steeper curve than a low-contrast film. Hi-con film would be used for titles or hold-out mattes. A low-con film, whose curve would be much flatter, might be used for a television-release print. In production, film stock with an average characteristic curve (angled at approximately 45 degrees) is commonly used.

The characteristic curve also indicates the film speed in its location on the scale. Two films can have the same contrast ratio but different ASA ratings. Relating this to a graph, the angle of the two plotted curves would be the same, but the horizontal position of the curve would be different.

The exposure latitude of a film is indicated by the curve's height from the beginning of the film's ability to change at low light levels to where it is unable to change with increasing light.

➡ The video equivalent to film's characteristic curve is the video waveform monitor set to display a frame of video without color information. Just as underexposing or overexposing a film increases or decreases the contrast, manipulating video levels does the same to a video signal.

The main difference between the waveform monitor and the characteristic curve is that the characteristic curve varies from film stock to film stock, depending on how the film was manufactured. The waveform monitor displays the recorded image or camera-created image, but the range (7.5 percent to 100 percent) of that image does not change. However, one can change the recorded image in playback mode and record that image, effectively altering the appearance of the original shot. See also *color correction.*

charge coupled device (CCD)

☐ A solid-state integrated circuit (chip) that converts light images into electronic impulses. The CCD has grown in sophistication and resolution and is now replacing camera tubes in many video cameras. It is a common element in home video cameras. It is lightweight and can produce pictures under very low light conditions.

➡ A film analogy to the CCD would be a combination of the film stock and the developing process. The CCD converts light to an electronic representation of that image. Developed film has converted a light image to a physical representation of that image.

checkerboard assembly

☐ An on-line editing session that conforms to an off-line work print using an edit decision list (EDL) and in which all edits from a single playback reel are completed before moving onto the next playback reel. See also *mode*.

➡ The process in film would be similar to that of a negative cutter who conforms a negative to the work print in order of ascending key numbers, probably an unpractical method in film.

checkerboard cutting

🎥 A method of editing every other scene onto an A and a B roll, for 16-millimeter negative cutting. Since 16-millimeter frame lines are not thick enough to allow an invisible hot splice, scenes are edited alternately onto two different reels for the lab.

➡ An analogy would be the building of A/B reels for an on-line editing session. Many industrial-program producers will build their shows on their own off-line editing systems but will have overlaps on the different reels for effects. The A/B reels are brought to the on-line session. One reel is used as a picture source until an effect is required, at which time both A and B reels are used. This situation also provides four possible tracks of audio for the on-line session, if mixing is going to occur during the on-line session.

≠ *Checkerboard assembly (B MODE)* is *not* the same as *checkerboard cutting.* A checkerboard assembly in video means that all the edits from one (or more) playback sources are recorded before putting up another group of playback sources. As the on-line editing progresses, the pattern of recorded picture looks very random, rather than a systematic, orderly checkerboard pattern. The entire checkerboard assembly process is precisely coordinated by a clean, computerized edit decision list.

chinagraph

🎥 A grease pencil used to mark the film work print, indicating effects and other editorial notations. The film is marked on the base, or shiny side.

➡ There is no standardized way to visually mark a video work print. However, occasionally a video note, created through the use of a character generator, is used during off-line editing to indicate missing effects or footage.

☐ **chroma**   Pure color, without gray or black. Some people use the term interchangeably with the word *color.*

chroma crawl

☐ A video aberration that occurs when two chromatic colors are adjacent on the television screen. At the meeting point of the two colors, an appearance of the colors crawling occurs as a result of the video process in which the signal has to quickly change from one frequency to another.

➡ Although the term *fringing* indicates a false coloration due to a defective optical system, the concept of inaccurate color representation is similar to chroma crawl.

chroma key

☐ The process of electronically eliminating a predetermined color from a picture (usually the background) and inserting another video source in its place. In most video productions, blue is used as the primary color for chroma keys. The most apparent use of a chroma key is the weather section of a newscast. The news person stands in front of a blue background. The blue is then electronically eliminated and the weather map is electronically keyed behind the weather person.

⇒ The film equivalent would be blue-screen process, although this film process is a little more involved than the video procedure. Mattes must be made of the blue-screen production material, then the background material is combined with the blue-screen footage in an optical printer.

chromium dioxide tape

☐ A tape stock made with particles of chromium dioxide rather than ferrous oxide. Chromium dioxide is a very high quality tape-stock material, referred to as *metal tape*.

⇒ The analogy would be a high-quality film stock, like Kodak's EXR series. The stock costs more but delivers higher performance.

cinch marks

☐ Sideways surface damage on videotape stock caused by improper handling, or damage caused by a poorly aligned capstan or pinch roller. See also *capstan*.

⇒ The film comparison would be scratches or other physical damage to the film stock due to misaligned equipment or improper handling.

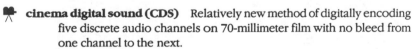 **cinema digital sound (CDS)** Relatively new method of digitally encoding five discrete audio channels on 70-millimeter film with no bleed from one channel to the next.

Cinemascope™

🎥 A trade name for a wide-screen process that employs anamorphic lenses to squeeze the image in production and then unsqueeze the image during projection. The compression/expansion ratio is 2:1.

⇒ The closest video analogy to Cinemascope would be high-definition television. With its wider aspect ratio, HDTV does offer a wider picture than the 4:3 ratio of standard television.

🎞 **circle of confusion** The area of a camera shot where the focus is acceptable although not technically in focus. In theory, there is only one clearly defined place behind the camera's lens where an image is perfectly in focus. However, the human eye assumes that the greater area surrounding the focus point, the circle of confusion, is also in focus. For the audience of a program to accept the focus of a shot, it must be within the circle of confusion.

circled takes

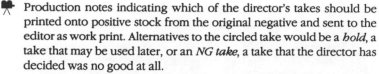

Production notes indicating which of the director's takes should be printed onto positive stock from the original negative and sent to the editor as work print. Alternatives to the circled take would be a *hold*, a take that may be used later, or an *NG take*, a take that the director has decided was no good at all.

In video production, there are often indications written in a script that a taped dress rehearsal or a particular read should be used by the editor.

clapsticks   A slate with a stick (usually hinged on the left side) showing the names of the director, cameraperson, and production company, the shot, and the take number, and used to visually identify a shot. The hinged stick is slapped down to produce a sound. This sound is used to synchronize picture and audio in the editing room.

Even though video records its production audio in sync with picture, clapsticks are often used during a video production to visually identify the take, shot, and other pertinent information.

claw   See *pulldown claw*.

clean edit   An edit that is technically flawless.

clean list

A listing of all the edits in a video program and corresponding information needed to perform those edits in an on-line editing session. Clean lists are often generated by a computer-cleaning program that analyzes all the sequential edit lists of a program and subsequently eliminates all unnecessary edits. It is assumed that a clean list is on some computer-readable format, usually a 5 1/4-inch floppy disk or a 3 1/2-inch or 8-inch disk.

The negative cut list is the film equivalent to video's clean list. The negative cut list is a carefully constructed listing of each shot and what key number that shot originates from. Negative cut lists can be created by hand. When a show is edited on a random-access system, the negative list is created by the editing system. Unlike the clean list, audio edits are not included in the negative cut list.

click track   An audio track with rhythmic clicks used as cues for music or rerecording sessions.

clip

1. To cut off. In a video situation, if an electronic signal is automatically cut off at a predetermined white level, it is said to be clipped. In an audio situation, clipping would indicate the cutting off of a piece of a word. See also *clipping; processing amplifier*.
2. A short section of film or video. Clips are used for reviews and news segments.

☐ **clipping** Electronically limiting video signals that are too high or too low. The device that does the clipping is called a *processing amplifier,* or proc amp. See also *processing amplifier.*

clogged head

☐ A video record or playback head that has a buildup of oxide or dirt that causes noise or loss of picture. A clogged head can also physically damage tape. A possible solution to this problem is to thoroughly clean the heads with a specifically designed cloth and cleaning solution. A clogged head can affect either the recording or the playback process.

⇒ The film playback method is to project an image through a lens. So, a parallel concept would be a dirty lens, which could alter the original image. During the filming process, a dirty camera gate, the point of exposure, can similarly result in a degraded image. Since the film dubbing process uses audiotape and record/playback heads, a clogged head can also be encountered in the dubbing process.

closed captioning

☐ A technical method of encoding subtitling information within a video signal. This embedded signal can be decoded, with the proper equipment, displaying written characters on the television screen. The purpose of closed captioning is to allow the hearing impaired to view a television program. The ⓒⓒ indication at the head of a program indicates that the program has been closed captioned. Some movies are being transferred to cassette (home video) with closed captions.

The encoded information is recorded in the vertical interval on line 21. The encoding process takes place during a dubbing process. The closed-captioned words and time-code cues are loaded into a computer. As the dub is being made, the time code triggers the computer to insert the encoded signal into the dub at the correct time. See also *vertical interval recording.*

⇒ Similar in concept, subtitling is a similar function in film production, although the purpose of the subtitling is more often to translate language. In practice, the projected print is made using an optical printer, the completed film elements, and art cards to create a new subtitled negative.

CMX™

☐ A company that developed one of the first computerized systems used to edit videotape. CMX was also one of the first manufacturers of nonlinear editing systems and has standardized and pioneered many aspects of post-production.

⇒ CMX is like many of the pioneers of the film industry that have survived the various twists and turns in the business of film production.

☐ **coaxial cable** Cable designed with two concentric conductors to carry picture and sound information. The cable that brings cable television into the home is coaxial cable.

CODE D6000
DATE SHOT: 2-18-91 (MON)

SCENE	TAKE	SOUND	CODE #	KEY #	DESCRIPTION	LAB ROLL
40	2	12	D6013 -6038	KK23 0975 9036→9060	W S MASTER - RUINI	E215-23
40A	2		6040-6081	9114→9154	MFS - PETERSON	
40B	1	↓	6088-6119	9162→ 9192	MCU - PETERSON	
40C	1	MOS	6120 -6141	9193→ 9215	INSERT - KNIFE	
	2	↓	6142-6155	9216- 9228	↓	
Color Chart		—	6156-6163	—		
40D	1	12	6172-6205	KK23 23 0975 9258→9291	MFS - GENERAL	
44	2	13	6207-6247	KTOS OS 2506 5327→5368	HI L MASTER	D215-24
	5		6252-6298	5463→5509	↓	
44A	2		6302-6364	5602→5664	CU — MIKE	
	5		6367-6432	5763→5827	↓	
44B	1	↓	6440-6493	5835→5888	INSERT	
Color Chart		—	6494-6499	—		
44C	1	13	6503- 6552	K7 38 2556 4960→5010	CU- CALAWAY	D215-25
44D	1		6560-6621	5016→ 5078	CU - STERLING	
44E	1		6625-6647	5083→ 5104	SHORT MASTER	
46	2		6651-6674	5141→5163	HI ANGLE MASTER (L.5)	
46A	1	↓	6677-6714	5166→5206	25 CALAWAY ↓ STERLING	

Figure 15 Page of a code book. The code book is a record of where the
original footage came from, its key number, and other vital information.

code book
 The code book, created and maintained by an assistant editor or editor,
is a detailed record of each take—the take's beginning and ending code
numbers, original negative key number, and a description of the entire
shot (Figure 15).

When the film dailies have been synchronized with each take's
respective audio, both the audio track and the film are coded with
identical sequences of numbers to facilitate keeping the separate tracks
in sync. If shots are misplaced or damaged, the code book is a vital tool
for finding shots or ordering replacement work print. See *coding*.

⇐ The video equivalent to the code book would be the master log book.
In certain productions, like multicamera shoots, the production assistant's
or assistant director's script serves as the equivalent of a code book. A
master log is a loose-leaf notebook that contains all information
concerning production footage and its corresponding time code.

In the case where the script serves as a log, usually multiple cameras
are used on a sound stage, for instance, in recording a sitcom. Here the
script contains the director's notes, selected takes, and camera angles.
The production assistant or assistant director often oversees the editing
process.

 code numbers   Sequential identification numbers applied by post-production staff to work prints and corresponding audio tracks for internal
editing purposes.

coding

🎥 The printing of identifying, sequential characters and code numbers on both the work print and the corresponding audio mag during post-production. This is done after the production audio has been synchronized with picture. Coding aids in keeping the previously unmarked film mag in sync with the picture even after the picture and track are cut into the work print. See also *key numbers*.

🔁 Since picture and sound have the same corresponding time-code numbers on videotape, a comparative situation would be recording time code on production footage after the shooting has been completed. See also *time code*.

🎥 **cold** The quality of light at the green or blue end of the spectrum. If a scene's color is toward that end of these colors, the scene is said to be *cold*. To *warm* the scene, one would either decrease the green or blue, or increase the red or yellow portion of the picture. See also *cold light*.

🎥 **cold light** A light that produces little heat and/or a light with little of the color red in it. For instance, a fluorescent light is a cold light. Cold light (bluer light) has a higher wave frequency than warm light. See also *color temperature*.

color analyzer

🎥 Also called **electronic analyzer**. A device that shines light through a film, reverses the polarity of the image, if necessary, and, through the use of a cathode ray tube, shows what a film image would look like if certain color correction methods were taken during the lab process of duplication (Figure 16). Such electronic forecasting is useful because repeated testing of actual film samples in the lab is relatively laborious, time-consuming, and expensive.

🔁 Video color is corrected during an on-line editing session. There usually is no previewing equipment, as in film, since the color correction that occurs in the edit bay is promptly recorded.

color balancing

☐ Adjusting the color components of a camera, an electronic device, or a playback source to meet a desired standard, such as matching flesh tones in subsequent scenes, matching cameras in a multicamera shoot, or just aligning a single camera.

🔁 The film equivalent could be ensuring that the same film stock, filters, and aperture are used in different takes or scenes or on a multicamera shoot. Another analogy is grading (color correcting) a film element.

color bars

☐ A test signal that is designed to be recorded onto a videotape to facilitate the alignment of that recording on a playback machine. The test signal may vary from facility to facility, but the purpose is the same: to provide a specific, standardized signal. Color bars are to video as tone is to audio.

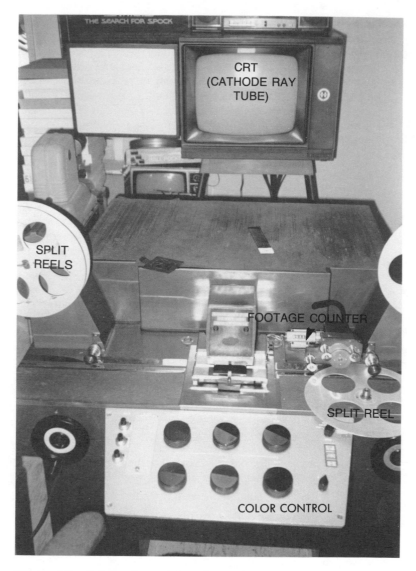

Figure 16 Color analyzer. The color analyzer uses a CRT to determine approximate color balancing for film processing. The dials in the foreground adjust the amount of color displayed on the CRT. Also note the split reels loaded on the left side of the machine and the disassembled reel laying on the right side of the console. Photo by Sean Sterling, courtesy of Cinema Research Corporation.

➥ A common test of a film printer's output is to regularly expose a standard piece of film to a test picture, often a laboratory aim density (LAD) patch. This film is developed and examined to insure that film duplication remains constant. Also, most optical houses and laboratories place one or two frames of a well-lit medium head shot of a person (referred to as a chinagirl) on the front of every film as a standard to judge the exposure of the film.

color burst

☐ The subcarrier frequency, located on the back porch of the composite signal, that is the frequency and phase reference for the color signal. This burst of electronic information carries the reference signal that tells the monitor what hue to make the color information that is included in the video signal. See also *blanking*.

➥ The film comparison would be the dye couplers and the exposed silver halides in exposed film. The dye, replacing the silver halides during film processing, locks the color and luminance information onto the film.

color correction

🎥 The use of a lens or filters to alleviate slight differences between the color temperature of a light source and the temperature that the film was intended to be used under.

➥ Most video cameras have a circuit that, on command, senses and adjusts the camera for either tungsten (artificial) light or sunlight. A white piece of material is placed in front of the camera, and a white-balance button is pressed. This engages the white-balance circuit and adjusts the camera's electronics as necessary.

☐ The process of altering the color of a scene or scenes. The shot is color-corrected either through the four controls found on a time base corrector, or, for more sophisticated luminance and color control, by using a device called a color corrector.

The time base corrector (TBC) has four controls designed to set up a videotape, similar to those found on a television set. There is a certain amount of range that can be achieved to alter the color of a shot. If more range is required, a color corrector is used. See also *time base corrector*.

➥ The film equivalent to video color correction is called timing or grading. This process takes place in the film laboratory. With the help of a specialized machine called a color analyzer, which reads assembled rolls of negative, the red, green, and blue components of each scene are viewed and assessed. Lab professionals and production staff determine the best density printing values of each color and the overall balance. These values are stored via a computer and used to conform the answer prints and final prints.

When transferring film to tape, there are two areas where color correction takes place. Usually the film-to-tape transfer device has the ability to adjust color and video levels during the transfer process. In many facilities, a second color correction device, a *secondary color corrector*, is installed for additional color control. See also *colorist.*

color corrector

☐ An electronic device that can manipulate color and luminance aspects of a video picture. Many color correctors can split the composite signal into its luminance and chrominance elements to allow for subtle adjustments. Color correction is a fundamental element of film-to-tape transfers and also takes place during on-line sessions of documentary and other location shows. See also *color correction; colorist; telecine.*

⇐ The film equivalent of a color corrector is the combination of an electronic analyzer (that previews color correction) and the printing system that alters the amount of light reaching the raw stock being exposed during the printing process.

⚙ The use of filters to convert the color temperature of light allowing the use of daylight film with tungsten lights and vice versa.

⇐ Video has an electronic sensing mechanism, called white balance, that can automatically adjust for different color temperatures when engaged.

☐ **color registration**   The superimposition of red, green, and blue to make a color television picture.

🎥 **color reversal inter-negative (CRI)**   A film stock once used in optical printing. The CRI is a negative created from another negative. The CRI eliminates the extra step of making a positive image of the negative and then another print onto negative stock. It has not been in use for several years.

✂ **color saturation**   The degree of absence of white in a color. The more saturated a color (the less white), the more intense that color appears. As more white is added to the color, the less saturated it would be. A deep red is a saturated color, while pink is basically the same color, only with proportionally more white.

color temperature

⚙ A measure of the color quality of light (not the heat radiated by it); the temperature of a standard black body at which a given color of light is produced. The higher the color temperature of a light, the bluer it is. Conversely, the lower the temperature, the redder the light. Measured in Kelvins, professional tungsten-halogen lighting is around 3200 Kelvins, while natural light at midday is around 6000 Kelvins. Note that, paradoxically, high-temperature blue light is labeled *cool,* and lower-temperature red light is considered *warm.* These descriptions are more associative and aesthetic than technically true.

Film is highly sensitive to color temperature and as a result, filters and even film stocks are manufactured to be used in certain lighting conditions.

➤ The video camera has a circuit inside it that can compensate for any given color temperature. And, since video production is more geared to recording either location news and documentaries or studio sitcom situations, the discussion of warm or cold lighting becomes somewhat obtuse.

News reports and documentaries are often limited to natural-lighting situations. Sitcom lighting directors often keep a similar lighting scheme throughout a set. Either way, the video camera's electronic circuitry can compensate the a scene's color temperature, when properly engaged. See also *white balance*.

colorist

➤ A person who transfers film to tape. Most often this person is highly skilled in adjusting the colors of scenes during the transfer. Many high-end colorists use flying spot scanners with sophisticated color correctors to accomplish the image transfer. See also *color correction; flying spot scanner.*

➤ The film equivalent is a timer or grader, the person who prepares the color balance (at a color analyzer) for the laboratory process. See also *timing.*

➤ The video equivalent is an editor who has color correction equipment and adjusts each shot for color balance. Color correction in video is less common than film grading. Many video shows have little adjustment to the original recording.

colors, complementary   Colors that are the result of subtracting a primary color from white light. These colors are yellow, magenta, and cyan. See also *subtractive color system.*

colors, primary   A set of colors within a color system, such as an additive system, that can be combined in various ways to create all other colors in a spectrum. Television, an additive system, uses red, green, and blue light. These primary light colors, when combined in equal amounts, produce white light. Film uses a subtractive system created by color dyes. Its primary colors are yellow, cyan, and magenta. See also *additive color system; subtractive color system.*

colors, secondary   The secondary colors of light are yellow, blue/green, and magenta. Secondary colors are created by mixing two primary colors. See also *additive color system; subtractive color system.*

comb filter   A process, inside a television monitor, adjusted to basic and harmonic frequencies, yet leaves intermediate frequencies unaffected. There are two common uses of comb filters. The first is to separate luminance (white levels) from the chroma (color) levels in a television receiver. The second use, in an editing bay monitor, is to reduce the ringing around small letters in video keys.

complementary colors   See *colors, complementary.*

☐ **component video signal**   A video signal that is split into luminance (the black and the white levels) and chrominance (color). These signals are carried and recorded separately. The component signal is ideal for sophisticated graphics and chroma key situations because the primary colors are also easily separated.

The three signals that are carried in a component video situation are the red value (R) minus the white value (Y) of the picture (R – Y), blue (B) minus white (B – Y), and just the white (Y).

The digital format D1 is a component signal, as are the Betacam™ and MII™ formats. However, Betacam and MII are often used in composite situations as well as component.

The three formats that actually record in a component signal (luminance signals are recorded separately from chrominance signals) are D1, Betacam, and MII. To edit in a true component situation, the entire editing room must be configured as a component room (three wires to and from each electronic piece of equipment), and each piece of equipment must be built electronically in a component configuration, including the switcher.

☐ **composite video signal**   A video signal that transmits or records luminance and chrominance as a combined signal. Most video electronics are based on composite video signals as it is less expensive than component wiring and electronics. See also *component video signal.*

☐ **computer assisted production switchers**   Video switchers that have a built-in computer that allows the switcher to store and execute complicated predetermined sets of effects with a press of a button.

☰ **computer enhanced graphics**   Images (drawings, photos, graphs, graphics, etc.) that are photographed by a camera, then manipulated by a computer and an operator.

There are many specific devices that are capable of manipulating graphics for video and film. There are several film devices specifically designed to electronically create images and then expose raw stock to the finished electronic image.

☰ **concave**   Curving inwards. A concave lens would curve inward, like a bowl.

☰ **condenser microphone**   A type of microphone containing two charged, adjacent plates, one of which is excited by sound (energy) entering the mechanism, altering the electrostatic charge between them. This continuous variation in the charge converts sound energy to electrical signals.

conforming
☰   The matching of original material to an edited work print.
☰   The matching of camera original film to the editor's work print. The matching is usually a matter of carefully following the key numbers on the work print. In some situations, the program has been transferred to

and edited on videotape. A list of all time code specifications for the video edits can be converted to key numbers and supplied along with a kinescope (a film copy of the videotape) work print. When no time-code-to-key-number conversion is performed, the film editor has to eye match the negative to the kinescope.

☐ An on-line editing session at which camera original footage is conformed to an off-line work print. In most cases, an **edit decision list** (EDL) is supplied with the work print to speed up and automate the on-line session. There are other instances where handwritten lists are used to conform original footage to a work print. Occasionally, an editor has to eye match each scene to conform camera original footage.

continuity   The consistency of all aspects of a character's clothing, action, and positioning, as well as the set details and anything that pertains to a scene. Since, in a single-camera production, all scenes in one location are usually shot at the same time but not necessarily in script order, it is the duty of the script supervisor to pay careful attention to those details. Polaroid pictures, extremely careful record keeping, and occasionally home videotapes are the tools of this person's trade.

Continuity also is a concern to a program shot in script order (like a live sitcom). However, because the action takes place in shooting order, continuity is not as big a concern as in single-camera production.

contrast

A comparison of the brightest portion of a picture to the darkest. A contrast ratio of 30 to 1 means that the most powerful light is 30 times brighter than the least powerful light.

Film has a much higher contrast ratio than video, and its contrast can be altered in the manufacturing process by flashing the film before production, by using certain filters during production, and by manipulating the image while timing the film in the lab.

Low-contrast film stock produces images with grayish blacks and dull whites. A high-contrast film creates sharply pronounced black-and-white images with the loss of midrange gray areas. High-contrast film would be used for titles or hold-out mattes. Low-contrast film is often used for television broadcast, although film-to-tape telecine is a more common route to video. See *characteristic curve.*

☐ Video's contrast, although considerably more limited than that of film, also can be altered. Lenses can be used to change the picture's contrast. Manipulation of the playback levels also can change the contrast of the picture. If the proper electronic gates are in place, the video signal can still fulfill the technical requirements of the electronics and not violate any broadcast policies. However, caution must be taken because the video signal can be rendered technically flawed without the proper equipment.

control track

☐ A pulse recorded at each revolution of the recording drum onto videotape during an assemble recording. Control-track pulses are used by machines during playback, recording, and other functions to maintain appropriate and constant servo speeds and to synchronize the video. All video recordings use a similar, yet not necessarily the same, type of control track. Low-cost editing systems count control-track pulses rather than read time code in order to perform edits and to keep track of tape location. Control track is only recorded in an assemble recording (usually made by pressing play and record simultaneously) on a record machine.

⇐ Film has sprocket holes. Control track is basically a form of electronic sprocket holes.

A similar signal in film with a very similar purpose is Pilotone, a signal that is generated at the film camera and sent out via wire to the sound recorder. This signal is a record of the speed at which the camera is operating at any point of time. Thus, the Pilotone is a control track of the camera recorded on audiotape. During the transfer of production sound from audiotape to magnetic film, a resolver continually adjusts the playback speed of the audio to match that of the camera when the film was exposed by reading the Pilotone.

convergence

☐ Within a color picture tube, the meeting of the three electron beams at the shadow mask.

⇐ The area on a screen where the focused light from the projector falls.

Convergence   Brand name of a commonly used video editing system.

core   The center of a split reel, a convenient type of film reel that can be split into two halves. The halves of the reel unscrew at the axle, allowing them to be taken apart. The film, wrapped around a film core, can then be removed and stored separately. This process eliminates the expense of having to purchase reels for each roll of film and saves storage space. Most editing situations use cores with split reels.

credit block   Informal term referring to the contractual credit information included at the end of movie trailers and movie commercials.

crop   To move in nearer or to mask or cut off. Usually the term is connected with art work—the cropping of a picture would be to mask or cut off a portion of the picture. When used in conjunction with digital video effects, it indicates the elimination of portions of the DVE rectangle.

cross talk   Also known as **bleed**. The running together, or bleeding, of one audio track onto another. This happens if an audio signal is very intense and the audio tracks are physically close to each other. This was a common occurrence in the early days of three-quarter-inch audio time code recordings. Currently, most three-quarter-inch time code editing is done using address track time code, which is located far from the production audio tracks.

☐ **crosshatch**   A video test signal used to align graphics and check the accuracy of a monitor. When using the crosshatch to align graphics, usually the art work is being photographed by a matte camera and positioned by hand. In the absence of a crosshatch, horizontal and vertical wipes are often used to check graphics for proper alignment and centering.

☐ **CRT**   See *cathode ray tube.*

crystal sync
    The locking of separate motors to a certain frequency. In order to achieve perfect synchronization between the film camera and audio tape recorder, that is, to keep the two unattached motors running at a constant, precisely equal speed, without having a wire connecting the two, an oscillating crystal is used to govern both the camera and tape recorder motors. In this manner, both motors are running at the same speed, although physically unattached. See also *Pilotone.*
    A similar video concept is house sync or gen lock. In a video facility, all electronic equipment is often in electronic time with a common signal. Video facilities lock their devices to a common electronic pulse, as opposed to a certain frequency.

cue   A prompt during a scene for a line of dialogue or some sort of action. The prompt can take many forms, including a director's call for action, a hand signal, or another actor's line.

cue card   A piece of cardboard on which are hand-lettered a performer's lines. The cue card is usually held either next to the camera or in the area into which the performer is supposedly talking, like near another performer.

cue sheet   A list of all the cues for a production. There can be separate cue sheets for lights, cameras, sound, exposures for printers, and so forth. The audio cue sheet is an important aspect of the dubbing, or sweetening, process. In this post-production audio situation, every sound in the project is noted, along with the footage at which this audio cue is to be introduced.

cut
    1. The immediate and complete change from one image to another. The cut is the most powerful transition used in all of picture editing. However, there are different practical methods of achieving the cut in film and video.
    2. A director's cue to stop the action in front of the camera; the opposite of *action.*
    The film cut is made by physically joining, or splicing, two separate pieces of film. The tape or butt splice is used for work-print editing. The cement splice is used solely for negative cutting as the splice is extremely strong and permanent.

☐ The video cut is made by electronically changing from one image to another during the vertical interval. The cut may be *recorded* (linear editing) or may be a playback function (nonlinear editing), or switched in a live, multicamera productions.

cutaway   A secondary image in a scene used to break from the focus of a scene or link the scene to a subsequent one. There are numerous opportunities in a scene to cut away from the main action.

Images used for a cutaway might be a reaction of an individual or a closeup of an object that is important to the action of the scene. Cutaways are also used to distract the audience in order to contract or expand film time, to cover a jump cut, or to use another angle or take. It is vital to take the time during production to shoot cutaways and anticipate editing needs and opportunities.

cutdown stock

☐ The unused tail end of an open reel of tape; the blank or black-and-coded stock left over at the end of a long videotape after a completed project has been edited. If a post-production facility's client does not want to buy the whole reel, the unused remainder is cut off and often sold to another client for a short project or used for another project of the original client.

⇐ The film equivalent would be the unexposed tail of a roll of film, the *short end*. Short ends are sold at a discount because they have been handled in varying degrees by a previous production.

cuts only

☐ An off-line or work-print editing system that does not have a switcher installed in the system. Without a switcher, the only transition that can be made is the cut.

⇐ The film editing of a work print is always configured as cuts only, as it takes an optical printer to create effects, and there are thus added at a later stage.

cutty   A scene or movie with too many cuts. This is an aesthetic judgment. Where one person might think that a commercial or program has too many edits, another might perceive that it is perfect. Different releasing mediums also require different methods of cutting. A music video intended for broadcast on MTV would use a different pace of editing than a documentary on classical music.

CYC   See *cyclorama.*

cyclorama (CYC)   A large, seamless, horizonless backdrop that is used on a stage to give the impression that the background is limitless; often used in commercials. Paper and cloth are used for temporary CYCs. Some CYCs are made of plaster and have curved bottoms where the floor meets the wall.

D1

🖵 A component digital videotape format that is 19 millimeters wide. More expensive than D2 or D3 since it records its information using three separate encoded signals rather than one, this method of recording and playback also makes for a more precise reproduction of the original signal. D1 is preferred for effects and graphics work. However, it requires specific electronic equipment with which to edit and/or duplicate. Although this gear is readily available, it has not been embraced as a widely accepted recording-and-playback format. See also *component video signal; formats.*

➡ A film analogy would be fine-grained 70-millimeter film.

D2

🖵 A composite digital videotape format, 19 millimeters wide, that stores its color information in one encoded signal; lower in cost than D1. Another advantage of D2 is that the maximum tape length is greater than the D1 format. D2 is the preferred editing and show format. Copying several generation produces almost no discernible signal loss, yet D2 is fully compatible with other standard video editing house equipment (switchers, DVEs, etc.). D1 has excellent capabilities for effects work and graphics recordings. See also *composite video signal; formats.*

➡ The film equivalent would be 65-millimeter film. D2 is in a commonly used configuration (composite video) and is of an extremely high quality.

🖵 **D3** A component digital videotape format that was developed by Panasonic and that offered a cost-effective alternative to D1, D2, and possibly one-inch. D3, with its half-inch-wide tape, is creating a demand because it is a digital format compatible with D2, has four channels of audio like the other digital formats, and, yet, is less expensive to purchase.

🖵 **DA** See *distribution amplifier.*

dailies

Prints of footage that a director has ordered during production; sometimes called rushes. These prints comprise the footage the director initially believes he or she will use in creating the final film. These dailies are often screened the day they arrive from the lab, usually the day following the shoot. Most often, dailies do not have sophisticated color correction. The lab determines an approximate color value for the scenes involved and prints everything at that color value.

Several steps of preparation are performed by post-production staff before dailies are ready for editing. First they are logged in, the audio is synchronized with the picture, and then the scenes are filed for editing.

The video analogy to dailies would be a *window dub*. A window dub is a video dub with a visual representation of time code "burned into" the picture as a reference. The window dub is usually on three-quarter-inch or half-inch VHS or Betamax format. Production staff assessments and off-line edit sessions would use the window dub to edit the program. There is no synchronizing of picture and audio necessary with video as there is in film.

daylight   Normal outdoor light measured at between 5500 and 6000 Kelvins. See also *color temperature*.

dB   See *decibel*.

dB meter   An instrument that measures audio levels calibrated in decibels. See also *decibel; VU meter*.

DDR   See *digital disk recorder*.

dead air   A time during a broadcast where no signal is being transmitted.

decibel (dB)   Unit of audio power measured on a logarithmic scale. One decibel is close to the lowest level that the human ear can hear. The measuring device used in audio recording is the volume unit (VU) meter. A volume unit is equivalent to one decibel. The 0 (zero) on a volume meter is a standard reference for record levels in the visual and audio industry.

decoder   Part of a television set that takes the incoming broadcast signal and turns it into an electronic beam aimed at the set's picture tube.

deflection coil

An inductor that produces a magnetic field and directs the electronic beam in a cathode ray tube.

The film equivalent would be the projector's lens that focuses the light onto the screen.

deflection yoke   An assembly of deflection coils for deflecting electron beams in a cathode ray tube.

◻ **degauss**
  1. To erase recorded material on videotape or audiotape by placing the tape near a powerful magnetic field. See also *bulk erase.*
  2. To electronically clean a television tube.

⬦ **depth of field**   A photographic term meaning the measured depth of the in-focus area of a scene being shot. The depth of field is measured from the nearest point from the camera at which an object is acceptably in focus to the furthest point.

detail
  ◻ A term that refers to the resolution of a particular shot. This resolution is determined by several factors, such as the light level of a particular shot, the camera's ability to record a shot, the number of times that shot has been dubbed, and to what extent the image has been altered in post-production through other enhancement devices.
  ➡ The film equivalent would be sharpness. In film, the sharpness is determined by the film's reaction to light as measured by its gamma, or contrast gradient, and its graininess (grain).

⬦ **diaphragm**   The movable shutter that creates the lens aperture opening. See also *aperture; f-stop; iris.*

⬦ **dichroic filters**   Blue filters designed to change tungsten light temperature to daylight color temperature. See also *color correcting; color temperature.*

⬦ **diffusion lens**   A filter that scatters light. Basically the filter bleeds light from the areas of highlights into the darker areas of the image. One of the results of using a diffusion filter is a loss of contrast, so they are often used in high contrast, bright-light situations.

⬦ **digital**   The manipulation or storage of information using ones and zeros. In electronics, a common alternative to digital storage or manipulation is in the form of varying voltages continuously proportional to the original signal; it is called *analog.*
  D1, D2, and D3 are digital video formats. One-inch, VHS, Betacam, 8-millimeter, and MII use analog signals for their operation.
  Digital video effects (DVEs) encode video to manipulate the signal. Digital disk recorders use digital encoding to maintain signal quality during multiple generational editing. Digital audiotape (DAT), compact disks (CDs), and digital audio workstations (DAWs) use digital encoding.
  Film is entering the digital domain also. High-end optical companies use sophisticated computers and unique software to create effects in a digital environment. Kodak's High Resolution Intermediate System is designed to eventually replace the optical printer as the creative device with which to create effects (Figure 17). The Post Group and Pac Title of Los Angeles have already developed the Gemini process for transfer-

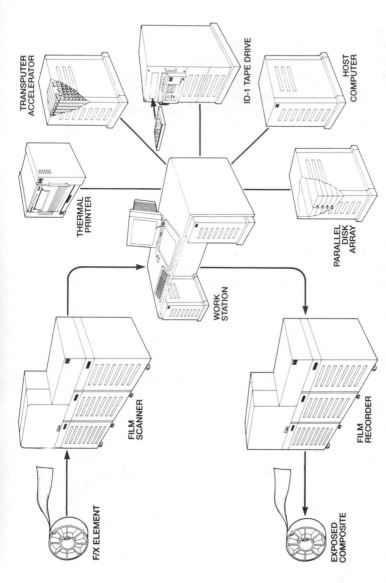

Figure 17 Kodak's High Resolution Intermediate System. Kodak has a film-to-digital-and-back-to-film system in development. There are several companies working on similar concepts in the feature-film optical area of electronics. Courtesy of Eastman Kodak Company.

ring video images to film. Employing computer-imaging techniques similar to those used in satellite-photo enhancement, the Gemini process has already been used for numerous feature-film effects. See *computer enhanced graphics.*

digital audio workstation (DAW)   An electronic device that uses digital audio rather than audiotape to combine sound sources. DAWs can be simple or complex, but they have become accepted mixing instruments in both film and video post-production (Figure 18). Advantages of DAWs over conventional mixing arrangements are quick slipping of tracks and the ability to hold several complex mixes within one device. Their main drawback is cost.

Figure 18   AMS AudioFile PLUS. The ease and speed of digital audio mixing has been used by both television and film productions. Shown here is the AMS AudioFile PLUS 16-output hard disk digital recording and editing system. Photo courtesy of the Neve Corporation.

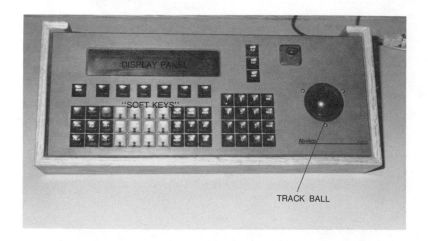

TRACK BALL

Figure 19   Digital disk recorder. Like most video equipment, the control panel of a machine relays commands to the actual operating equipment, often located in a machine room. Here is the control panel for an Abekas A-62 Digital Disk Recorder. Note the trackball on the right side of the Liquid Crystal Display window in the center, and the soft key just below the display. Photo by Sean Sterling, courtesy of Video Research Corporation.

digital disk recorder (DDR)

☐   A computer processor-driven device utilizing a magnetic disk to store, manipulate, and reproduce digitized audio and relatively limited amounts of video (Figure 19). There are DDRs designed for audio mixing and completely different DDRs for video work. The video DDR is a device that has the ability to record multiple generations of video without any discernible signal loss. Before the advent of digital videotape formats, the DDR was the only way to build complex effects that required multiple recordings.

The DDR can record single frames of video and can play back video at variable speeds from 0 to plus or minus 30 times sound speed. (A VTRs maximum variable speed is three times sound speed.)

Another purpose the DDR serves is to record single frames of video in pin-registered film-to-tape transfers. Many pin-registered transfers pull the film down one frame at a time, and then the DDR is used to record the frame. When the DDR is filled (the maximum it can hold is 110 seconds), the video is recorded on videotape. See also *layering*.

A DDR designed for audio can also record many generations without a signal loss. Some disk systems are equivalent to a multitrack recorder, offering many tracks and mixing capabilities, Digital audio is rapidly being used in both film and video sound work.

⇐   The video DDR's use of hold-out mattes, recording multiple passes, and extremely fast variable playback speeds make it most similar to a film optical printer. However, a single DDR has a time limit of 50 seconds onto which it can record for the purpose of layering.

digital sync

A method of synchronizing a camera and sound recorder whereby the camera sends a signal to the recorder for each exposed frame. This signal is then used to synchronize picture and sound after the film has been developed. See also *crystal sync; Pilotone.*

Video records its audio in sync with picture. However, a similar concept is house sync or gen lock. In a video facility, all electronic equipment is often in electronic time with a common signal. Where crystal sync is the locking of several separate motors to a certain frequency, video facilities lock their devices to a common electronic pulse. This process is used in multicamera situations and video post-production facilities.

In a situation where a multitrack audio source needs to be locked to video, time code can be a synchronizing element in the post-production process.

digital video   A video signal encoded in electronic units of ones and zeros. Rather than representing a video signal through continuously varying voltages (Figure 20), like analog technology, digital processes divide a signal into extremely minute units of time, measure the signal strength within each time unit, and then represent that strength in numeric code. The main advantage of digital recordings is that with each successive

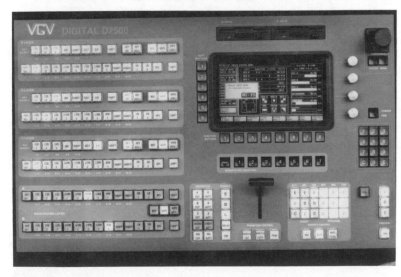

Figure 20   VGV digital video switcher. As digital video has become accepted by the production and post-production community, switchers and other video devices have been developed. Shown is one of these devices: the VGV 2500, a composite digital switcher. Photo courtesy of VGV, Inc.

generation, there is little or no signal degradation. Since the picture information is a numerical series of ones and zeros, the video can be duplicated exactly as it was in the original. There are three commercially accepted digital video recording formats currently in use in the United States: D1, D2, and D3. D1 is a component signal in which three wires carry the video signal with the luminance separated from the chroma. D2 and D3 use a component signal in which the video is carried on one wire.

There are several other forms of digital video. A DVE device (Abekas A-52, Kaleidoscope, ADO, etc.) converts video into a digital signal in order to manipulate the image's size and position. A video paint system also converts video into a digital signal in order to perform its painting functions. A digital disk recorder (DDR) converts video into a digital signal. The DDR was one of the first digital editing devices available. See also *digital disk recorder; formats (video)*.

digital video effects (DVE)

A generic word that indicates the manipulation of the information composing a frame of video through the use of a special electronic processor. The word also is a generic term for these electronic devices that perform a digital video effect. There are several types of DVE devices and types of moves available through these devices. Some of the more popular devices in current use are the Ampex ADO, Abekas A-53, Mirage, Pinnacle, and Kaleidoscope.

The DVE converts the analog video signal into a digital form to allow the manipulation of the image, then converts it back to an analog video signal. Hi-con images can be used in DVE devices to refine the electronic hole-cutting feature of the device.

Typically available DVE moves are zooming in and out from or to anywhere in the video raster, mirror imaging (flips), repositioning of the video rectangle, and/or zooming past normal size. Most increases in normal size are limited to 4 to 8 percent due to the limitation of the digital device's video expansion capability.

Other effects that may be available, depending on the particular device being used, are matting (using a hi-con to cut a hole in the video background), tracks and trails (video echos) either within the key signal or outside the signal, the ability to turn the video like a page, warping the picture into various geometric designs, and slicing through another DVE rectangle.

The optical printer is the DVE of film. It is within this device that most film effects are created. Like the DVE, the optical printer does not create images, but manipulates a shot's position and appearance within the frame.

dimmer   An electrical device that reduces entering voltage to a light, thereby controlling the intensity of illumination. Care must be taken when using dimmers in production because lowering the intensity of the light also changes the color temperature of the light.

dimmer banks Groups of dimmers located in the same location.

DIN exposure index

An exposure index designating a film's relative sensitivity to light. The DIN index is logarithmic; each progression of three degrees represents a doubling of film photosensitivities. The alternative ASA exposure index is arithmetic. Table 2 compares the ASA and DIN exposure indices. DIN is a standard developed by a German organization and used particularly in Europe. See also *ASA exposure index.*

The stock in videotape does not determine the light levels required for an image recording. It is the camera's pickup tube or CCD that determines the light sensitivity. This is most often expressed in the number of foot candles required to create a picture.

There are different levels of videotape stocks that have progressively fewer dropouts, better reception, and superior retention of electrical signals. Metal tape is more sensitive and a higher quality tape, but it costs more and should be used with a compatible tape machine. Broadcast-quality tape has fewer dropouts than consumer videotape.

direct positive print A positive-film print made without a negative. This type of film was used a great deal in news production before video became the primary television medium. Much of the reason for use of direct positive film is to bypass printing from a negative.

directional microphone A microphone that picks up sound only from the direction in which it points. A commonly used directional microphone is a shotgun microphone. See also *cardioid microphone; shotgun microphone.*

director The person who controls all aspects of the action in front of the camera. This includes the lighting, actors, camera movement, and any other movement that is intended to be in the frame. The film director is extremely dependent on the camera operator for judgment of technical aspects such as focus and composition. Although the use of video assist allows the film director instant access to the results of a particular shot, this technology costs money and is not available to every production.

Table 2.   ASA–DIN Conversion Table

ASA	DIN	ASA	DIN
50	18	200	24
64	19	250	25
80	20	320	26
100	21	400	27
125	22	500	28
160	23	650	29

The video director has the ability to see the shot as it occurs. However, the video director often has to deal with many cameras rolling at once. This operation of choosing shots often rests in the control booth where the director instructs the technical director on which shot is to be fed to the master tape or to a live broadcast feed. In some cases, there are multiple record machines rolling for protection.

In both cases, film and video, the director is not just a leader on the set. A director is a person who has the ability not only to get a project underway but also to keep it rolling until the project is completed. The skills involved in being a director reach much further than visualizing a script and also include the roles of a politician, confidant, and general.

The director is in charge of the crew as well as the completion and vision of the project.

Generally, the film director works in front and around the camera, while the video director first works on the floor with the actors, then retires to the studio booth or mobile unit to instruct the camera crew via headset. Because of the serial nature of many television productions, the director in film tends to have a much greater aesthetic impact than the television director. Television production parameters and style often are largely established by the producer at the show's inception, and individual directors on specific episodes generally adhere to these guidelines.

dissolve   A transition in which one scene fades out as another fades in. The dissolve is a commonly used effect to denote a change in time or location. The film dissolve is created in the optical printer, the video dissolve through the use of the switcher. See also *on-line*; *opticals*.

distribution amplifier (DA)   Device to amplify video and audio signals. The DA is often used to create multiple outputs from one source. DAs are also found in sound facilities.

dock   Scenery or equipment storage area.

Dolby™   A trademarked audio noise-reduction system, developed by one of the original inventors of videotape, Ray Dolby. The concept behind the Dolby system is to push the audio levels higher during recording and then to lower them during playback plus *notch* a portion of the high spectrum where tape hiss is found.

There are a series of Dolby noise-reduction systems. Dolby A is a professional system that splits the audio spectrum into four frequency bands. Dolby B is a domestic system used for audio cassette tape and FM radio. Dolby C is a recent domestic system for audio cassettes with more noise reduction than Dolby B.

Dolby SR (Spectral Recording) is an extremely high-end Dolby encoding and decoding process that is designed for a wider dynamic range of sound. With the large speakers necessary in a film auditorium, the ability to play quiet audio, such as a whisper, at loud volume can cause problems because the system noise on the sound track is also increased in volume. Dolby SR removes a great deal of this unwanted noise, allowing for louder playback volumes in quieter passages.

dolly

1. A wheeled platform, sometimes mounted on tracks, that offers untroubled, smooth movement of the camera. A dolly can range from an inexpensive mount, totally unsuited to deal with bumpy ground, all the way to being a sophisticated camera mount with built-in shocks and motorized movement.
2. A shot that has camera movement in it (a dolly shot or a tracking shot).
3. The actual movement of the camera ("Dolly in to a close shot.").

dolly shot   See *dolly*.

dominant color   The prominent color in a picture or scene. The term could be used for either film or video; however, it is more often used in film.

double

To record over. Doubling is also used in audio post-production, meaning that the rerecording is additive to the original recording and does not erase it.

An actor who takes the place of a star during dangerous stunts.

double action   The duplication of an action or part of an action, usually as a result of a continuity error in editing or production. See also *continuity*.

double exposure

The exposing of a single piece of film to two different images. The two images could be superimposed or could fill areas held from exposure by mattes.

The video comparison would be an effect created in the switcher containing two or more images. Many times, either numerous playbacks are used to create these types of effects or multiple passes are made using D1, D2, or a digital disk recorder.

double printing

Optically slowing down film action, accomplished by printing each frame a multiple of times. The same basic effect can be achieved in production by speeding up the film as it goes through the camera. If the shot is planned to be slowed down, usually the film is overcranked, that is, shot at a faster than normal speed. However, a protection shot at sound speed also is usually made. See also *opticals; overcrank*.

The video equivalent would be motion control, also called variable speed playback. The most obvious and frequent use of variable speed playback is during sports broadcasts.

Digital disk recorders (DDRs) like the Abacus have even more range, up to 30 times sound speed for both forward and reverse.

Videotape variable speed is limited to three times forward, one times reverse.

double splice   Taping both sides of a taped edit, most often done before projecting a work print. The double splicing helps keep the pieces of film from being separated by the projector. See also *tape splice*.

double system

A production method in which the sound and picture are recorded on separate mediums. There are film systems that record audio directly onto a magnetic stripe on the film. This method was used for news production; however, videotape has almost completely eliminated film as a production medium for television news. Almost all film production is double system.

The challenge in a double-system recording is to keep the audio in sync with the picture. There are several solutions to this challenge, the most sophisticated being the use of crystal sync on the motors of both the camera and audio recorder.

In post-production, double system requires at least two synchronized strips of film—one for picture and one for sync sound. With multiple-plate flatbed editing systems, editors can be working with up to four separate strips of varying configurations (three picture, one sound; two sound, two picture; etc.).

Video productions in which multitrack recordings are made would be an equivalent to double system. This type of production, most often used in concert situations, is one in which sound is recorded separately from picture. During post-production, the picture and sound are reunited.

downstage   A stage term for movement toward the audience, away from the back of the stage. The term is also used in live sitcom productions, as the program is performed much like a play.

downtime   Time when equipment is taken out of service for maintenance or repair. During a production, downtime is extremely costly since the crew waits around for the equipment to be replaced or repaired.

dowser

A shutter used to block the light beam in a film printer or projector.

The fader bar on a switcher performs a fade to black.

dress   To add props to a set; to dress up a set.

drop frame time code   When time code was originally introduced, time code ran at a precise 30 frames per second. However, the color video signal actually is projected at 29.97 frames per second. For a short program, this error of 0.03 frames per second presents no problem. However, this difference translates to 3.6 seconds more time code than program over the span of an hour (Figure 21).

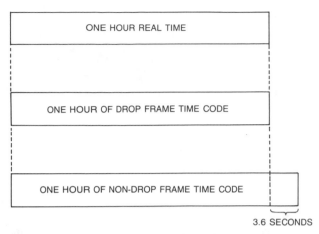

Figure 21   Time code comparison. Drop frame time code is an accurate representation of time. An hour of calculated non-drop frame time code will be 3.6 seconds longer than a true hour.

To alleviate this potential problem, drop frame time code was introduced as a standard references system by the SMPTE. It is called drop frame time code because two time code *numbers* are dropped every minute (*except* at each ten-minute mark). This effectively eliminates the time discrepancy between the time code and the actual program length. Note that the numbers are dropped, but the picture remains totally intact.

In summary, non–drop frame time code is not time accurate, but drops no numbers; drop frame time code is time accurate.

drop shadow

A black shadow that separates a title or image from the background. The shadow is often designed to give the impression that a source of light is creating a shadow. The directional source of the light can change the side on which the shadow appears to be.

The drop shadow is actually created by the hi-con or hold-out matte when the background is transferred in the optical printer. The title, being processed in the optical printer, will not cover the whole area of the hold-out matte.

The drop shadow can come from either the electronic machine that creates the image, like an animation system or character generators, or from a switcher, which can create a drop shadow in any keying situation.

dropout

An area on videotape that is missing oxide and, thus, can have no picture or audio information recorded there. Although these areas are usually small, picture and/or information can be lost. The aberration usually appears as a silver or black horizontal streak on the tape. Severe dropouts may interfere with adjacent scan lines and produce repetition of lines or even signal breakup. Dropouts may be the simple result of defects in tape stock or may be produced by mishandling or malfunctioning equipment. Most professional video machines have electronic devices called dropout compensators to help mask video dropouts.

⇐ The film comparison would be a scratch on the film. Another comparison would be hair or dust in the film gate that subsequently affects the image on the film.

dropout compensator

☐ In most professional videotape playback machines, electronic devices that sense a dropout (the lack of oxide on the tape) and insert the previous line of video for the missing picture information.

Tapes that have excessive dropouts are not only extremely poor recording mediums, but can also severely damage the video playback machine by depositing their oxide into the machine's delicate transport mechanism.

⇐ The film equivalent would be a liquid gate. This process of shining light at a film surrounded by a liquid that essentially fills scratches is a close comparison to a dropout compensator.

drum

☐ A cylindrical wheel around which videotape is wrapped in order to record or to play back that tape.

⇐ The film equivalent would be the camera or projector gate. This is where the film is placed in order to expose or project that film.

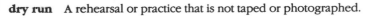 **dry run**   A rehearsal or practice that is not taped or photographed.

dub

1. To make a copy of audio on magnetic film (mag) by using a machine called a dubber.
2. A copy of audio on mag. A dub could be made for many reasons, from making a copy for the sound editor to sending a copy of production audio for the creation of radio or television commercials.

☐ 1. To make a copy of a reel or section of a reel onto another piece of tape.
2. A copy of a videotape. There are several levels of dubs. A window dub, for work-print editing, is not color corrected nor intended for broadcast. Yet a dub made of a show master may be of a high quality and intended for delivery.

dub mode

☐ The ability of several brands of three-quarter-inch video recording decks with specific output and input channels to transfer radio frequency signals without converting the signals into a video signal and back again. This method of recording in dub mode is not used for editing as no effects can be performed. However, for duplication, this method of recording saves some signal loss, which can be an advantage in this type of format.

➡ The best comparison for this feature would be a dupe of a 16-millimeter film that is made using a step optical printer, which intermittently exposes film frame by frame, ensuring a high-quality dupe.

dubber

 An audio recorder and/or player that makes copies. The dubber is a long vertical machine with supply reel, take up reel, and an audio stack capable of reading the audio on the film mag. A dubber is used in the audio-mixing (dubbing) process of film post-production. The dubber plays back one full coat magnetic film (mag) that can hold up to four tracks of audio.

➡ The four-track tape recorder is the closest video machine to the dubber since the dubber can read a maximum of four tracks. Video-audio post-production most often employs more than four tracks.

dubbing

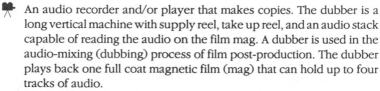 1. Any transfer of sound, usually employing the use of a dubber.
2. The final audio post-production process phase, in which all sound effects including ADR, Foley, dialogue, music, and production tracks are combined (mixed) together. The process is one of putting up all the sound effect reels on machines called dubbers. The number of dubbers is directly related to the number of tracks that are to be mixed together. They could include such tracks as effects, music, dialogue, ambient sounds, and ADR tracks.

The dubbers are rolled simultaneously and the audio sources are mixed together while a copy of the picture is viewed. The multitude of tracks is most often reduced to four tracks of audio: dialogue, music, effects, and narration. Usually one film reel at a time goes through the dubbing process. Once that reel is completed, another set of tracks are loaded onto the dubbers.

➡ The video equivalent is called *sweetening*. Sync production sound is recorded on a multitrack recorder/player. On other tracks are recorded music cues, effects, ADR lines, Foley effects, and additional dialogue. The tracks are cleaned of unwanted audio, placed in relationship to the picture, and finally mixed down to four distinct tracks as in film mixing, the standard four tracks being dialogue, music, effects, and narration.

▢ The process of making a dub (copy) of a videotape. When a tape is copied from one format to another, the show or image is said to have been bumped. ("Bump the three-quarter-inch to one-inch.").

➡ The film comparison is to make a dupe (short for *duplicate*), to make a copy of a piece of film. This process is accomplished through the use of a printer, and then the dupe is developed in the lab.

dubbing stage

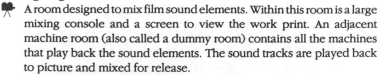

A room designed to mix film sound elements. Within this room is a large mixing console and a screen to view the work print. An adjacent machine room (also called a dummy room) contains all the machines that play back the sound elements. The sound tracks are played back to picture and mixed for release.

➡ The sweetening room is video's solution to mixing sound. In the sweetening room is usually a monitor or television to view a three-quarter-inch dub of the program, a mixing console, and a multitrack audio recorder. Recently, digital audio workstations (DAWs) have become common in the sweetening room.

dupe   Also called *duplicate*.

1. A print created from an internegative or a duplicate negative.
2. A black-and-white print on reversal stock.
3. The action of making a dupe print.

➡ Although there is no reversal printing process in video, the dub is probably the closest equivalent. A video dub is a copy of another videotape, but the copy is always a positive image.

duplicate   See *dupe.*

DVE   See *digital video effects.*

DX

Abbreviation for *double exposure and dissolve.*

➡ In a video edit decision list, the letter D indicates a dissolve.

dynamic microphone   A microphone that uses the variations that sound waves cause on a moving coil of wire and a magnet to capture sounds. They are inexpensive and sturdy.

dynamic tracking

A method of playing back videotape at a variable speed and still keeping the picture stable enough for broadcasting. Not all tape players have this ability.

➡ The film equivalent would be an optical printer capable of step printing. See also *printer.*

E to E See *electronics to electronics*.

EBR See *electron beam recording*.

edge numbers

The sequential combination of numbers and letters used to identify frames on the film. Edge numbers are printed on the base of the film when the film is manufactured and are visible once the film is developed. Edge numbers occur every 64 perforations (the equivalent of 16 frames or every foot) on 35-millimeter film and every 16, 20, or 40 frames in 16-millimeter film.

Negative stock loaded into a camera directly will have increasing numbers as the action progresses. However, edge numbers on negative stock that has been rewound before use will decrease as the action progresses. Separate sets of numbers called code numbers can be printed onto rush prints and work prints for later reference in editing and negative cutting.

The video equivalent is time code. However, time code does not have the numerous variations that edge numbers do and, thus, has the possibility of being used more than once during production or even on the same reel. The purpose is similar to that of key numbers though, to identify every frame on a videotape.

edit

1. To carefully build a program from sections of film, videotape, or both to tell a story. Although the actual process of building the program is distinctly different in the two mediums, the ultimate purpose is the same: to produce a satisfying program by presenting only the most relevant portions of the available footage.
2. To join two specific segments of film or video. Also, the point at which these segments are joined.

☐ **edit black** Also called **video black**. Preparatory signals recorded continuously over the length of videotape, enabling it to be used for editing and insert recording. Specifically, these signals include stable video, control track, and, occasionally, time code. The stable video signal is video black.

edit decision list (EDL)

☐ A schedule of video edits, each defined by time code, that specifies the form of a program (Table 3). An EDL can be computer generated or hand written on log sheets. For each edit, the list includes source reel information, beginning and ending time code of each video segment, and duration of the edit. Computerized edit decision lists also include record tape time code in-and-out numbers. More sophisticated EDLs can also include complicated switcher effects and can trigger information for firing other peripheral editing equipment such as character generators and DVEs.

⇐ The code list created for the negative cutter that is copied from the footage of the work print. There are also indications of effects on the work print. See also *banner*.

edited master

☐ The final edited version of a tape program. This tape could include all picture information including effects and titles, or it could be a final version of an effect or segment.

⇐ The timed internegative, that source from which the prints are made, would be analogous to the edited master. This is the final program with approved audio mix and grading (color balance).

editor

⚞ A highly creative individual whose responsibility it is to cut together footage shot during production. A good editor will often increase the impact of the production, as well as offering alternatives in pacing, shot selection, and juxtaposition of shots and scenes, and can also save a bad project. The film editor is responsible for sound as well as picture and often oversees one or more assistant editors.

☐ The job of a video editor is essentially the same as a film editor but is more machine oriented. Thus, the number of people on a video-editing crew tends to be smaller than on that of a film crew. The sound-editing process, referred to as sweetening, is not usually considered part of the editing domain.

In some cases, the audio of a program is finished in the on-line editing session. In this situation, the on-line editor also becomes the mixer, combining music, effects, and sync dialogue while picture is also conformed. This eliminates the necessity of finishing audio at a sweetening company.

⚞ Although *film editor* and *videotape editor* are most common, there are many other types of editors and editing titles, as in the following

Table 3. Edit Decision List

THE *VIDEO ONLY* CUT (FOR ONE SECOND)

edit	#	mode	transition duration	source in	source out	record in	record out
1	V	C		01:00:15:11	01:00:16:11	01:00:00:00	01:00:01:00

A *VIDEO ONLY* DISSOLVE

(**A** side of effect: two seconds, **B** side: three seconds, dissolve for fifteen frames. Note that the effect is included in the running time, and, therefore, only two seconds and fifteen frames are fully visible of the B scene.)

edit	#	mode	transition duration	source in	source out	record in	record out
1	V	C		02:00:15:11	02:00:17:11	01:00:00:00	01:00:02:00
1	V	D	15	04:10:25:22	04:10:28:22	01:00:02:00	01:00:05:00

TAIL FILM NOTATION EQUIVALENT HEAD

A *VIDEO ONLY* FADE-IN

(Note that this is a fade from BLK;BLACK to a source with an edit duration of five seconds.)

edit	#	mode	transition duration	source in	source out	record in	record out
BLK	V	C		00:00:00:00	00:00:00:00	01:00:00:00	01:00:00:00
1	V	D	15	04:10:25:22	04:10:28:22	01:00:00:00	01:00:05:00

TAIL FILM NOTATION EQUIVALENT HEAD

A VIDEO WIPE ALSO DISSOLVING ON AUDIO CHANNEL ONE

(Note the number next to the "W" indicating a specific number of a wipe. This number usually relates to one switcher manufacturer's code or even to one model of switcher. Also an "audio" wipe will be an audio cross fade.)

edit	#	mode	transition duration	source in	source out	record in	record ou
2	B1	C		02:00:25:22	02:00:30:22	01:00:00:00	01:00:05:00
1	B1	W001	15	04:10:05:00	04:10:10:00	01:00:05:00	01:00:10:00

TAIL FILM NOTATION EQUIVALENT HEAD

WIPE Soft #5

A CUT ALL AUDIO CHANNELS

edit	#	mode	transition duration	source in	source out	record in	record out
1	B	C		01:00:15:11	01:00:16:11	01:00:00:00	01:00:01:00

examples: sound editor, effects editor, dialogue editor, Foley editor, ADR editor, news editor, trailer editor, documentary editor, feature editor, on-line editor, off-line editor, music video editor, sitcom editor, episodic editor, and so on.

EDL   See *edit decision list*.

effects (EFX or FX)

Generically and broadly, any component of the picture or sound that is not a simple production element and is specially created to imitate a natural or unnatural event or otherwise produce some unusual response within the audience. Effects can, thus, be a part of production (makeup effects, for example) or added later in post-production, as are many sound effects and visual effects (dissolves and fades, for example).

Effects for both video and film can be grouped broadly into sound/audio effects and visual effects.

1. SOUND/AUDIO EFFECTS

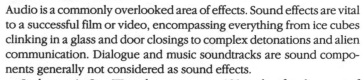

Audio is a commonly overlooked area of effects. Sound effects are vital to a successful film or video, encompassing everything from ice cubes clinking in a glass and door closings to complex detonations and alien communication. Dialogue and music soundtracks are sound components generally not considered as sound effects.

In the movie *Star Wars*, there were over 180 tracks of audio, most of which were effects. Effects can come from a variety of sources: actual audio recordings, Foley work (Figure 22), and sound libraries. One of the unusual factors about sound effects is that the sound making an effect and how it appears to sound in a production can be totally different. Many sound effects are manufactured by taking existing audio sources and altering them through variable-speed playback, audio equalization, and/or reverberation. See also *effects track*.

2. VISUAL EFFECTS

There are some basic production and post-production techniques employed in many visual projects. Below are several often used techniques. See also *on-line*, *printer*.

3. PRODUCTION EFFECTS

Lighting.

Probably the most commonly used film effect, the manner in which a scene is lit often creates the mood and feel of the scene. The lighting director has many tools at his or her disposal from a variety of lights to colored gels.

Video also uses lighting but, in most cases, it is not nearly as sophisticated as in film productions, mainly because the budgets in video are not as large as those in film.

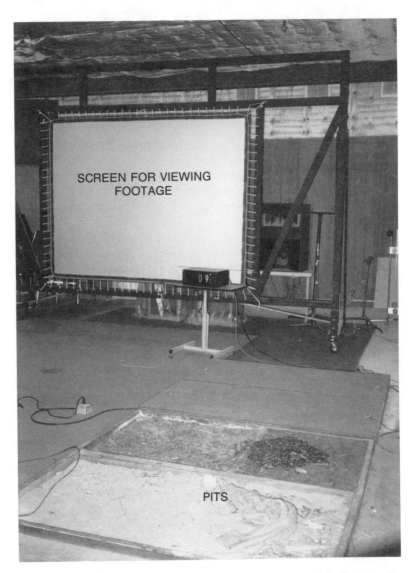

Figure 22   Foley stage. The Foley stage is used to create sound effects. As the film is projected on the screen, Foley artists re-create sounds to match the action. Note the pits filled with various material in the foreground. Photo by Sean Sterling, courtesy of Cinesound, Hollywood, CA.

Camera and lens movement.

The dolly, crane, tracks, and zooms are used to create effects on the movie screen. Although camera movement for its own sake is annoying and distracting, selective use of these devices can be dramatic. Alfred Hitchcock used the simultaneous *dolly out and zoom* quite effectively.

Video production uses camera and lens movement; however, zooms and pans are more common than dollys and trucking movements.

Motion controlled camera.

The ability to make precisely repeated camera movements has allowed filmmakers to use miniatures and blue-screen effects where camera movement must be repeated over several setups.

Video does not use motion control cameras to the extent that film does. However, the ability does exist.

Over cranking, under cranking.

Slowing or accelerating the rate at which film passes through the gate creates either a slow-motion effect (over cranking) or a sped-up effect (under cranking). Slow motion shooting, or over cranking, often is used in conjunction with a stunt or shot that cannot be easily repeated, such as a large explosion.

Video has the capability to record in over- and under-crank mode; however, it takes a special camera and recorder for very high speed or very low speed video recording. Most effects of this type are created in post-production either by using variable-speed video playback machines or by employing a digital disk recorder (DDR) for the variable-speed effect and recording the result on tape. The DDR has a higher playback speed (up to 30 times sound speed) than most variable-speed tape players.

Pyrotechnics.

The destruction of a set is often used in film making. Careful attention must be paid when explosives are used on a set. Both video and film employ these types of effects.

Miniatures.

These scale models have come into their own since *Star Wars.* Where once these effects were considered cheap and ineffective, it is now a fact that a carefully constructed model can be an impressive addition to a film project.

Video production also takes advantage of miniatures but not to the extent that filmmaking does.

4. COMBINATION PRODUCTION AND POST-PRODUCTION EFFECTS

Blue screen.

This film process takes place on the set and in the optical printer. The actor or object (perhaps a miniature) is shot in front of a blue background. A suitable background is then shot. The two images are combined in an optical printer. Part of the intermediate step in the post-production process is creating a hi-con image from the blue-screen footage. This provides the optical printer with a hole that prevents the area where the actor is to be from being exposed.

The video equivalent of blue-screen production is chroma key. The background that will be electronically eliminated can be any color, although blue is used most often. Through the use of a switcher or other chroma key device, production and background footage is combined. In some cases, a holdout matte (explained in the following paragraphs) is created for further image compositing.

Mattes.

The matte is a high-contrast film element used to mask off sections of the film frame while optical work is occurring within the optical printer. Mattes are used in creating titles on film and compositing matte paintings, blue-screen effects, and split-screen effects.

There are two uses (and technical explanations) of the video terms *matte* and *hold-out matte*. In one case, a matte is a key (an electronic insert) filled with a switcher generated color, such as a white title card with text subsequently colored blue by matting.

The second use is similar to the film usage. A hold-out matte (high-contrast video image, usually a black-and-white) is fed into the switcher and used as an external key cutter. This image cuts the key into the background video; then another video source fills that hole.

So in video, the hold-out matte is different from the matte.

5. POST-PRODUCTION EFFECTS

The optical printer is one of the main image-manipulation devices used in creating film post-production effects. In most cases, there are at least two film elements involved in making an effect in an optical printer. For instance, a simple dissolve requires three elements: a film stock (the destination stock) to expose, a scene that is dissolved from, and a scene that is dissolved to. In the example of creating a title, there are also three elements: the original title footage, the hi-con (to prevent the film stock from being exposed where the title will be), and the background scene. In more complicated effects (multiple miniature shots, like a series of spaceships), there can be over ten film elements combined in the optical printer to create a single shot.

Besides combining film elements, the optical printer is also capable of creating wipes, dissolves, fades, and slow-motion effects. In all these cases, the effect is created using production footage, the optical printer, and raw stock to photograph the printer's effect.

The video analogy of the optical printer is either the switcher or graphics system. The switcher is the heart of a video editing bay and performs many standard video effects (wipes, dissolves, keys, mattes). In the editing bay, video is combined in the switcher and sent onto the record machine.

In the case of a video dissolve, there is a *from* scene and a *to* scene. The switcher performs the transition from one source to the other. See also *A/B roll (video)*.

In titling situations, the graphics are keyed. They may come from an electronic typewriter (character generator), a picture recorded on a videotape, or from a camera shooting an art card or other photographic source.

Video graphics can create or enhance titles, graphics, rotoscoping, and animation. In these cases, each individual frame is input into the device (sometimes called a paint system), treated as required, and then recorded back onto tape. Logos, graphics, and very complicated commercial animation are common uses of graphics systems. See also *on-line; printer*.

effects track   An audio track with sound effects only, without music or dialogue. In complicated film mixes, groups of audio effects are often mixed down to one track to speed the final dubbing session. In video on-line editing sessions, it is not unusual to record sound effects on a track separate from dialogue. Separating the effects and dialogue can help the audio mixer speed the sweetening process. See also *dubbing; sweetening*.

EFP   See *electronic field production*.

EFX   An abbreviation for *effects;* used in script notations.

Ektachrome™   Brand name of a positive film stock manufactured by Kodak.

electrician   A technical-crew member who moves and places lights and electrical connections. The electrician works under the supervision of the lighting director (often called a gaffer).

electron beam

☐ A stream of negatively charged particles aimed at the front of a CRT that excites phosphors on the face of the tube.

⇌ Analogous to the electron beam is the rectangle of light that travels over the audience from the projector.

electron beam recording (EBR)   A high-quality, tape-to-film transfer process found in flying spot scanner telecine devices. An electron beam generated by the videotape electrical signals sequentially traces the images onto film. The flying spot in this type of telecine device refers to the electron beam acting as a light source and thereby exposing the film.

electron gun

☐ A cathode at the small end of a CRT that produces a defined beam of electrons that scans the face of the tube. This is the stimulation that makes the phosphor-covered face of the CRT glow, creating a picture. The beam is aimed by the deflection coils.

➡ The light source in the film projector is the film analogy to the electron gun.

electronic analyzer   See *color analyzer.*

electronic camera

▢ A camera that focuses an image onto an electronic conversion device (either a pickup tube or CCD) that converts that image into electronic impulses.

➡ The film camera has a purpose similar to the electronic camera and has the ability to focus an image onto a conversion system. It happens that the film, via its photosensitive emulsion, is not only the conversion device, it is also the storage medium.

electronic editing   The selective process of piecing together a program using video and/or digital video equipment. Electronic editing can be either linear or nonlinear (random access). In linear editing, edits are recorded one by one from source reels onto destination tape as the decisions are made. In nonlinear editing, an editor uses computer processors to preview, make, and modify decisions out of sequence, developing a continuously updated edit decision list within the computer's memory. The EDL is not implemented and no video is recorded until the editor decides the list is final. See also *edit decision list; linear editing; nonlinear editing.*

electronic field production (EFP)

▢ Location videotape recording; often referred to as ENG (for location news shooting) or just EFP, if it is material other than news.

➡ Location production is the film equivalent. Although film is not used for news gathering as much as in previous years, location production still uses 16-millimeter film cameras for documentaries shot on location.

▢ **electronic news gathering (ENG)**   Basically, a term that refers to the use of video news cameras on location.

electronics to electronics (E to E)

▢ An electronic mode, found on many video machines, that puts all the electronics into position as if the device were actually in record. This mode is designed for setting record levels for video and audio without having to actually go into record.

➡ Although the film printer has no setting like E to E, the color analyzer performs in an E to E type of mode. Colors are previewed and fine tuned in the analyzer before actual exposure in the printer.

emulsion

▣ The chemically active portion of film that preserves the photographic image. The emulsion side of the film is the dull side. The shiny side is the celluloid backing.

The emulsion consists of gelatin and silver halides—the gelatin is used as a suspension medium and the silver halides react to light. When the halides are struck by light, they break into two components: halogen and a metallic silver deposit. During the film's processing, the unexposed silver halides are washed off the film, leaving the metallic silver grains.

In color film, there are three separate layers that make up the emulsion: the yellow-dye layer, the magenta-dye layer and the cyan-dye layer. It is the combination of these three colors that produces the negative image. The dyes in negative film are the complementary colors cyan, magenta, and yellow.

Although the video camera *converts* the physical image into electronic pulses, it is the oxide on the videotape that stores these pulses. The comparison to the film dyes would be the pickup elements found inside all video cameras. Since video is a positive recording image, the primary colors of the light spectrum (red, green, and blue) are used to re-create the encoded picture.

ENG   See *electronic news gathering.*

ENG camera   A lightweight video camera used for location shooting.

enhancement   Improving the apparent definition of a picture. There are devices used in video post-production that can reduce film grain and sharpen the edges of the image. See also *image enhancement.*

EQ   See *equalizer.*

equalization   The process of adjusting sound frequencies. Equalization is used to strengthen or alter weakened signals due to the nature of audio recording. Other reasons for equalization are the adjusting of the sound quality for aesthetic reasons, changing the sound for a particular feel, or matching another mixer's equalization. .

equalizer (EQ)   A device that separates particular frequencies of sound and then allows these frequencies to be controlled individually. This type of equipment can be used to improve certain aspects of sound (dialogue, effects, music, etc.). Tape hiss or other offending sounds can be reduced; bass, or low end, sounds can be removed or increased as the script requires.

The *parametric equalizer* (Figure 23) utilizes dial controls to adjust frequency alteration as well as the range of the frequency area being changed. This type of device provides more control over the equalization process. The *graphic equalizer's* sliding pots (potentiometers) offer a visual representation of the amount of equalization, but the bandwidth of frequency alteration is limited to the slider's built-in specifications. Both types of EQs are found in film and sound mixing studios.

Some video editing bays have equalizers built into their audio mixing boards. However, if there is an audio (sweetening) session

PARAMETRIC EQUALIZER   TIME CODE GENERATOR   TIME CODE READER

Figure 23 Parametric equalizer. A parametric equalizer installed in a rack. The four large dials each control different ranges of frequencies. Also note the time code generator and time code reader located below the equalizer. Photo by Sean Sterling, courtesy of Video Research Corporation.

following the editing session, it is a common practice to record the audio from production sources flat, that is, without any sound alteration. A sweetening room has more varied and powerful audio devices than a video editing room.

erase head   A rotating electromagnetic element in a videotape recorder that erases previously recorded material before the tape reaches the record head(s). The erase head is also referred to as a flying erase head because it is not stationary but rotating on a drum along with the record head(s).

exciter lamp   The sound head's light source for optical sound track in a film projector.

exposure   To subject a photosensitive material to light. In film, the photosensitive material is film. In video, the photosensitive material is a pickup tube or a CCD.

exposure factor

An adjustment of the iris opening of a camera to compensate for light-absorbing or light-reflecting material put between the subject and the lens, such as a filter. See also *T-stop*.

Since the video image can be seen and monitored on test equipment during the recording process, adjustments can be made immediately for light-absorbing or light-reflecting material put between the subject and the lens.

exposure index   A number assigned to a film stock indicating that film's relative sensitivity to light. The index is based on the film's emulsion speed, a standard exposure, and specific processing conditions. A film's exposure index is expressed with a number. See also *ASA exposure index; DIN exposure index.*

exposure meter   A device with a photoelectric cell that measures the intensity of reflected light. The photoelectric cell can be made of selenium, cadmium sulfide (CdS), silicon blue, or gallium photo diode (GPD). See also *CdS meter.*

EXT.   The abbreviation for *exterior*, used extensively in scripts. See also *exterior.*

extension tubes   Cylinders and/or rods that are added between the camera body and the lens to move the lens away from the camera for special, close-up work. These devices are often used in commercial work where extreme close-up photography is often used.

exterior   A simulated or actual outdoor scene.

external key cut

☐ A high-contrast video signal sent to a switcher and then used as a pattern to cut an electronic hole in a background. External key cuts can be provided by character generators and digital video effects devices, or videotape. High-contrast holdout mattes provided by a video paint system are another source of external key cuts. The hole created in a background video by using an external key is normally filled in with video from another source.

➡ A high-contrast (hi-con) **holdout matte** is the same as an external key cut. The film hi-con, though, usually has a male and female counterpart, each to protect one area or the other from exposure within the optical printer.

F-stop   The ratio of the focal length of a lens to the diameter of the lens opening, and, thus, a unit of measure for the lens opening, or aperture. This formula represents a standardization that allows one to know exactly how much light is falling onto the film or photosensitive mechanism. Each successive f-stop is a doubling or halving of the amount of light admitted to the film through the aperture. The ten standard f-stops are: f1, f1.4, f2, f2.8, f4, f5.6, f8, f11, f16, and f22. See also *T-stop*.

fade-in   A gradual transition from black to picture. In film, a fade-in is created by running film through an optical printer. The iris on the printer is opened at a predetermined rate, thus fading in the image. A piece of virgin film stock is exposed to this process and developed.

In video, a fade-in is identical to a dissolve and in computer dialogue is actually called a dissolve. A video source is played back, and the image is dissolved from black to full picture at a predetermined rate. The output of the switcher is fed to another tape machine, and the effect is recorded.

fade-out   A gradual visual transition from an image to black. In film, a fade-out is created by running film through an optical printer. The iris on the printer is then closed at a predetermined rate. A piece of virgin film stock is exposed to this process and developed.

In video, a fade-out is identical to a video dissolve and in computer dialogue is actually called a dissolve. A video source is played back, and the image is dissolved from full image to black at a predetermined rate. The output of the switcher is fed to another tape machine, and the effect is recorded.

fast lens   A lens that admits large amounts of light to pass through it. Thus, a fast lens allows a cameraperson to use a lower ASA film stock (creating less grain and greater contrast ratio) or to relatively shrink the iris (creating a larger depth of field).

fax   A machine that transmits and receives printed information via phone lines (a *facsimile* machine).

FC   See *foot candle.*

feed reel   The reel that is the source of film or audio- or videotape in either an open-reel configuration or a cassette.

feedback

A generally undesirable electronic loop of audio, being continuously intensified, creating a high-pitched squeal. An example would be a microphone connected to an amplifier that in turn is connected to a speaker. If the microphone is next to the speaker, sound will come out of the speaker and return to the microphone, be amplified, and the audio creates feedback.

A video machine recording its own output will create feedback, it is in an endless loop. Occasionally, unusual effects can be created with feedback.

Both of these situations are similar to placing two mirrors facing each other. The image (sound) is repeated continuously.

feet

A common film reference term for *duration.* Reel lengths are described in feet rather than actual running time. Equipment is designated by feet. A 35-millimeter metal reel comes in 400-, 1,000-, or 2,000-foot lengths. A 1,000-foot reel of 35-millimeter film is 11 minutes running at sound speed (24 frames/second, 16 frames/foot). See Table 4.

Videotape length is described in time. Physical tape length, in inches and feet, is rarely discussed.

fiber optic   A clear plastic material used to transmit optical signals. Fiber optics are becoming more and more common in computer and tele-communication networks.

field

1. One half of a single television frame consisting of every other scanline of video information. Two fields make a frame.
2. A production location: "Go out into the *field* and shoot the show."

On location, rather than being in a studio or shooting out on the back lot.

Table 4.   Film-to-Feet Conversions

One Foot of Film	Equals	Frames
35 millimeter	=	16
16 millimeter	=	40
8 millimeter	=	72

fill

🎥 Old, unneeded film used to temporarily replace audio tracks to maintain sync with picture in areas where soundtrack is missing. See also *leader*.

➡ Used stock that is kept in a facility to make B reels and other recording chores not requiring pristine virgin stock. See also *slug*.

film

🎥 A narrow, thin, flexible, transparent substance (like cellulose) coated on one side with a thin layer of photosensitive material. Film is manufactured in various formats and sensitivities, from X-ray film to feature-film stock.

➡ The comparative item is videotape; a thin ribbon of a substance like plastic that is coated with a thin layer of easily magnetized material. Videotape is manufactured in various formats and qualities from consumer half-inch to metal digital videotape.

film base

🎥 A transparent, strong, flexible cellulose ribbon coated on one side with light-sensitive photographic emulsion.

➡ The base in videotape is Mylar, and, although it is required to be strong and flexible, it does not need to be transparent.

🎞 **film chain** An older term for the equipment used to transfer film to videotape through the use of an optical multiplexer. See also *optical multiplexer, telecine*.

🎞 **film clip** A short section of film (even if recorded on videotape). Film clips are used for reviews and news segments.

🎥 **film loop** See *loop*.

film plane

🎥 That point behind the lens where the film is momentarily placed during exposure. Ideally the film plane is at the same point at which the rays of light reflected from the subject are focused by the lens.

➡ That point inside the video camera where the light converges on the pickup tube or CCD; called the target.

film speed

🎥 1. The sensitivity of a film's emulsion to light. A portion of the film is tested for its sensitivity before sales begin and the degree of sensitivity is indicated by an exposure index usually expressed in **ASA** or **DIN** standards. See also *ASA exposure index; DIN exposure index*.

As a rule, the more sensitive a film stock the larger the film grain. This grain is more apparent because of the larger grain size. When pushed to its limits, a high-speed film may take on the appearance of boiling.

➡ The video comparison to film speed is the light level requirements of the camera pickup tubes or CCD (a CCD requires less light than a pickup tube). If a video camera is used with less than adequate light, the result could be unwanted and potentially unacceptable video noise.

Video noise is equivalent to the increased grain apparent in low light/high speed film stock.

2. Speed, in number of frames, at which film travels past the picture gate. See also *opticals*.

➡ In almost all cases, video passes across the recording heads at a constant speed. Playback-speed variations can be made during the editing process, but most recordings are created at sound speed. See also *drop frame time code*.

film strip

A short section of film (usually 35-millimeter) designed for single-frame projection. Film strips are an inexpensive method of producing and distributing educational and informational programming.

➡ Video disks are also used for one-frame-at-a-time projection. A video disk can be programmed to go to specific frames when interfaced with a computer. Certain brands of video disks are also capable of recording stereo audio, as well as playing individual frames at various speeds, including sound speed (30 frames per second).

film-to-tape transfer Transferring film images to videotape. See also *film chain; telecine*.

film weave See *weaving*.

filter The process of eliminating specific elements (frequencies, noises, aberrations, etc.) from the whole. Electrical, electronic, optical, and audio devices are used to strip the offending portions from the whole. Camera filters are used extensively during film and video production to modify the color of the light striking the photosensitive medium or device. Such filters often are used in combinations and referred to as filter packs. See also *equalizer, image enhancement*.

fine cut

A work-print version of an edited program that is either the final version or very close to being the final version. The difference between the rough cut and the fine cut is one of selective elimination and the addition of copies of opticals. The rough cut will have whole takes and occasionally multiple takes. The fine cut will have eliminated duplicate shots and unneeded heads and tails of individual takes. The pacing of scenes and scene placement are altered and refined. Whole sequences are often deleted.

As opticals are created in the film lab, dupe copies of the footage are inserted in the fine cut. In addition, copies of selected stock footage and second unit footage are included in the fine cut.

➦ Usually all video work-print tapes are called rough cuts. Often each progressive edit is numbered in ascending order along with its completion date. The first edit might be called *cut one*, and so on until the final cut is achieved.

first generation

🎥 Camera original footage, either negative or positive.

☐ Original videotape recording.

🎥 **fish-eye lens** An extremely wide-angle lens, used for special effects, either during production or in film post-production.

🎥 **fishpole** A long shaft or stick that is used to extend the reach of a microphone. The fishpole provides the capability to place the microphone immediately above the performers, just out of sight of the camera. See also *boom*.

🎥 **flashing** The procedures of intentionally and precisely exposing film to a low level of light before or after production, but before processing. If a negative stock is flashed, the relative strength of the black is reduced. If print stock is flashed, the relative strength of white levels is reduced.

🎥 **flat** Stretched canvas or other cloth nailed to a wooden frame. Flats, which originated in the theater, are often used as false walls.

flatbed

🎥 One of the most flexible film editing machines. It is an editing and viewing device that is built on top of a table. Laying flat on the table are plates designed for film (both picture and sound) take-up and source reels. At the back of the flatbed are one or more screens for viewing footage. The plates are motorized and can be run in sync together or separately.

This motorized editing tool has speeded up the editing process and allows the editor to work on a flat surface (versus a vertical format with the Moviola).

Recent advances allow audio and picture to be automatically synchronized by reading time code on both the audio and picture time code tracks. There are also optional devices that allow for quick film-to-tape transfers.

The alternative to using a flatbed would be to use an upright Moviola or hand-operated synchronizer (gang).

➦ The equivalent of a flat bed would be to use a computerized off-line editing system, either a linear or random-access editing machine. These systems are sophisticated, and many have the ability to memorize switcher (optical) settings, to clean edit decision lists, and to operate numerous and varied videotape machines.

🎥 **flip** A revolving effect. In film, the optical printer is used to squeeze one image into the center of the frame and then reveal a new scene. In video, this process is accomplished through the use of a digital video effects device. See also *on-line; opticals*.

flop over
- To reverse the screen direction in a scene. See also *flip*.
- Video post-production would use a DVE device in the on-line process to mirror image a frame or series of frames.

flutter   An audio or video term indicating a flaw in picture or sound with unwanted variations in frequency.

fly   To suspend off the ground.

fly space   The area above a stage where scenery and curtains are hung.

flying spot scanner   A type of film-to-tape transfer system that employs a focused beam from a CRT tube to illuminate film in a precise scanning pattern. The resulting image is broken into primary light colors and then picked up by three video tubes. This configuration allows for accurate reproduction of the film image and a great deal of control over the color on the finished videotape. See also *electron beam recording*.

focal distance   The length between a camera's lens and the point of focus of the subject. This is the distance measured ever so carefully by the assistant cameraperson in order to maintain the closest possible focus.

focal length   The distance from the center of the lens to the light's convergence point (focal point) behind the lens.

focus puller
- The first assistant cameraperson; the individual responsible for the control of focus during filming, as well as the maintenance of the camera.
- The camera operator is responsible for focus, mainly because the operator is capable of seeing whether the shot is in focus and because there is less movement of the camera in video production.

follow focus   To keep an object in focus as it moves in front of a camera.

font   A type style of a particular design and size. In the case of film, fonts are found on title cards. Video fonts come from title cards, character generators, and paint systems. See also *character generator; on-line; opticals; titles*.

foot
- 1.   A measure of film length. See also *feet*.
- Videotape duration is described in running time (hours, minutes, and seconds) rather than feet and frames.
- 2.   The end of a reel of film.

foot candle (FC)   A measurement of light equivalent to that produced by one candle at the distance of one foot. See also *lighting; lumen*.

footage

- The length of a scene measured in feet.
- All the visual production material of an individual program or scene.

 forced development A use of increased time or temperature in the development process of film to adjust for underexposure of the original film during production. Certain looks or effects are always attempted during the production phase. Other ways to affect the film image would be through the use of filters or flashing the film. See also *filter; flashing; pushing film.*

foreground

1. The closest part of the shot to the camera. See also *background.*
2. In an effect, the part of the effect that appears to be on top.

 formats The available sizes of film or videotape (Table 5).

FILM
Film production uses several formats. The formats for most professional uses are either 16 millimeter or 35 millimeter.

super 8
A home-use format. Also a practice format for beginning filmmakers. Because of its small size, minimal professional support, and low image quality, it is not considered a professional format.

16 millimeter (16mm)
Developed in 1923, 16 millimeter began as a home-use format, but since then, improvements in cameras and film stock have brought this format into the feature arena. It is used in documentary production as well as television and motion picture production. However, in many cases, super 16 has replaced standard 16 millimeter for television and movie shooting. Note that 16 millimeter has the same projection speed as 35 millimeter (24 frames per second), but has 40 film frames per foot (versus 16 for 35 millimeter), and, therefore, runs at 36 feet per minute.

Table 5. A Brief Comparison Summary of Camera Original Footage

Film	Video
8mm	VHS, Betamax, 8 mm
16mm	three-quarter inch, SVHS, Hi8
35mm	Betacam, MII, one-inch
65mm	D1, D2
70mm	HDTV

Note: These are general comparisons, not meant to be hard and fast rules.

super 16

This format uses 40 percent more image area than regular 16-millimeter film. It does this by utilizing the area delegated for the sound track. It also has the same aspect ratio as 35 millimeter. However, in order to use super 16, it must be blown up to 35 millimeter or transferred to video because there is no room on the film for sound.

35 millimeter (35mm)

This is the established format for feature-film production. This format has been highly developed and is extensively supported. There is even a format (Vista Vision) that exposes the film sideways in order to achieve its wide-screen effect. Note that 35 millimeter has 16 frames per foot and runs at 24 frames per second, or 90 feet per minute.

70 millimeter (70mm)

Rarely used in production, with the exception of specialized wide-screen projection, 70 millimeter is used often as a releasing medium. For the most part, though, 70-millimeter release prints are usually blowups from 35 millimeter.

VIDEO

The video world also has numerous formats (Table 6).

consumer formats

The consumer-format wars are continuing. First there was Betamax, then VHS, then 8 millimeter, then Hi8 and SVHS. All have advantages and disadvantages. Suffice it to say that, properly used, these consumer formats, with the proper equipment, have been and will continue to be used in off-line editing systems.

Only SVHS and Hi8 have the potential to be used in broadcast situations; however, care must be taken when these formats are used in industrial and broadcast purposes.

three-quarter-inch format

Three-quarter-inch began as an off-line format and quickly gained widespread acceptance in broadcast news departments and for nonbroadcast information programs.

The advent of Betacam and MII displaced three-quarter-inch as the high-end news format, but many local stations still use three-quarter-inch. It is also a format for point-of-purchase displays (POP) and is still extensively used for off-line.

one-inch formats

In the 1980s, one type of one-inch format was embraced by the broadcast community. Called *Type C*, this one-inch-wide tape and its equipment became the workhorse of commercial production and post-production video. Miles of it are used daily for television broadcasts and up scale industrial productions. Currently it is the industry standard.

There is another one-inch format: Type B. Although delivering a picture superior to Type C, it did not become the established commercial type of recording that Type C did. There are still facilities that use

Table 6. Formats

Half-inch Formats

---

8 millimeter	consumer home video
VHS	consumer home video
Betamax	consumer home video
Super VHS	consumer home video and some broadcast uses
Betacam	broadcast programming
Betacam SP	broadcast, off-line
MII	broadcast

Three-quarter-inch Formats

Three-quarter-inch U-matic	industrial production, broadcast, and off-line
Three-quarter-inch U-matic SP	industrial production, broadcast, and off-line

One-inch Formats

Type A	not in use any longer
Type B	limited broadcast, high-end industrial
Type C	broadcast, high-end industrial

Digital Formats

D1	high-end graphics, telecine mastering
D2	high-end broadcast, industrial recording and editing
D3	high-end broadcast, industrial recording and editing

Two-inch Format

First video recording medium. Not in wide use any longer.

Type B, yet most of these companies will use it in conjunction with Type C.

digital video
Quickly gaining in popularity are the three digital formats: D1, D2, and D3. All use a digital recording and playback function that allows for many more generations before signal loss is noticed. D1, a component

recording medium, is superior to D2 and D3 but is more expensive to purchase. Besides having shorter tape length, it requires a complete component video path in order to take advantage of D1's power. This type of wiring can be extremely expensive when a complete edit configuration or electronic rack is considered for rewiring.

The D2 and D3 formats are less expensive as they utilize a composite recording signal (one wire output for the video signal) and can be integrated quickly and easily into an existing (and more commonly found) composite editing situation (Figure 24).

two-inch format
The original videotape format rarely used in video production today. One-inch replaced this behemoth as the broadcast standard. The smaller one-inch format was easier to maintain and less expensive to purchase.

 FPS   See *frames per second.*

frame
 Adjusting the camera so that the required action appears in a specific portion of the picture.
1. One rectangular image within an exposed piece of film.
2. The alignment of projected film so that the frame line will not be visible in the viewing device.

Figure 24   Sony D2 digital video machine (a digital video record/playback machine). The slot at the top of the picture is where the cassette is inserted into the machine. Photo by Sean Sterling, courtesy of Video Research Corporation.

➡ The comparison would be the adjustment of the vertical control of a monitor or television set.

☐ Two interlaced fields of video comprise a frame. So, there are two rectangular images that comprise a video frame. See also *scanning*.

frame bar   See *frame line*.

frame line

➡ Also called **film bar**. The narrow strip of film that lies between exposed frames. This is where the film is cut for editing purposes.

➡ The video equivalent is the vertical interval—that space of time between the display of one field and the next. During the vertical interval, framing pulses and other encoded information (closed captioning, VIRS, VITS) are sent.

frame rate   The number of frames per second that are being displayed (Table 7). The frame rate can be altered during production or in post-production. The frame rate may be altered during production to achieve a specific effect, but it must be planned carefully. Usually, the frame rate is kept at sound speed (24 frames per second) during production and then altered as required in post-production. By speeding up film as it goes through the camera, the action is slowed down. By slowing down the film speed, the action is speeded up. See also *overcranking; undercranking*.

There is a push from some film makers to increase the standard film sound speed from 24 frames per second to 30 frames per second. There are two reasons to increase the film frame rate. The first is to increase film resolution—thirty frames per second is 20 percent more images per second than 24. The second is there are a great deal of music videos and commercials being shot at the rate of 30 frames per second, images destined to be viewed on television. With the 30-frame rate, there is no duplication of fields as necessary when transferring a 24-frame rate to 30-frame television. See *three-two pulldown*.

Table 7.   Frame Rate

Format	Frame Rate
Film sound speed	24 frames per second
Alternate film speed	30 frames per second (occasionally used for U.S. broadcast commercials. See three-two pulldown.)
NTSC video	30 frames per second (Actually 29.97 frames per second. See *drop frame time code*.)
PAL video	25 frames per second

▢ The number of frames per second at which video is shot or replayed (Table 7). For most applications, video is shot at 30 frames per second. There are stop-motion video record machines, as well as editing devices that are specifically designed for recording video animation. However, in most video playback situations, the playback frame rate is altered for any effect that requires a speed that differs from the standard speed of 30 frames per second.

All video playback machines have limitations as to how fast or slow the machines will play back an image. The other limitation to whether a video machine can play back in other than sound speed would be whether the tape machine has a dynamic tracking capability. This allows the picture to be viewable and a technically acceptable picture for broadcast and/or duplication. See also *effects; on-line; opticals.*

▢ **frame store**   An electronic device that stores one or more video frames in memory. Some frame stores are designed to hold thousands of frames of pictures while others are designed to accept moving video, store one frame, and then feed that frame into a video system, in electronic time with the rest of the system. Frame stores designed for running video are often used to synchronize signals from remote locations with studio broadcasts. Frame stores are sometimes used in place of a time base corrector. Repeated use of a frame store can delay the picture enough to throw the picture out of sync with the audio.

frames per second (FPS)
🎥 The rate of speed at which film is shot or projected; usually kept at sound speed (24 frames per second).
▢ The rate of speed at which videotape is shot or replayed; usually kept at 30 frames per second.

🎥 **freeze**   A hold on one frame of picture. A film freeze is created in an optical printer by exposing a series of destination frames to one frame of source footage. A video freeze can come from a variety of sources: a videotape machine with dynamic tracking, digital video device, paint box, or frame store.

fringing
🎥 Faulty color reproduction due to a flawed or misadjusted optical system.
⇐ The video comparison would be video ringing or chroma crawl, although these effects are often a natural occurrence in color reproduction within a video system.

▢ **front porch**   The part of the horizontal synchronizing signal between the leading edge of the blanking pulse and the leading edge of sync. See also *blanking.*

🎥 **front screen projection**   Casting of images onto a highly reflective surface from the front (viewer) side; usually a film procedure.

full coat

A film stock used for audio recording whose width is completely coated with oxide. Full coat is usually delivered at the end of a dubbing session. On the full coat would be four mixed tracks: music, narration, dialogue, and effects. The optical track for the finished film is created from this full coat. Full coat is also used if tracks are mixed down to save the mixing process time. See also *magnetic film*.

The video comparison would be a four-track audiotape because the maximum number of tracks available on a full coat is also four tracks. However, the audio system for post-production is usually working with multitrack audiotape, which often deals with at least 24-track audiotape.

FX

Abbreviation for *effects*, interchangeable with the abbreviation EFX; used in script notations.

Within the computerized edit decisions list is a series of symbols that equate to certain standard effects: D is for dissolve, W for wipe, C for cut, and K for a key. See also *edit decision list*.

G – Y (G minus Y)   The green color television signal (G) minus the luminance (Y) signal. This signal is an encoding for the composite video signal made to keep the signal path to one wire. See also *component video signal; composite video signal; Y*.

gaffer   The head lighting technician for a film or television program. The gaffer is responsible for consulting with and carrying out the plans of the Director of Photography. This includes adjusting lights as well as taking care of the power requirements of the set.

gain control

The control on an audio device that raises or lowers the record, mix, or playback signal strength.

A control that adjusts white levels on a video camera (not to be confused with opening the iris). On a video time base corrector, this adjustment would be called a video control adjustment, and on a television set, brightness control.

Although the film camera cannot adjust its white levels during actual shooting, it is the film's sensitivity to light that compares to the gain control of the camera. This sensitivity is reflected in a particular film's characteristic curve. See also *characteristic curve*.

gamma

The contrast gradient of a film, representing the particular relationship of the light and dark areas of images developed upon it. Basically, it is the measure of the angle of the straight line in the film's characteristic curve as compared to the fog level. This is a figure that expresses the film's contrast. See also *characteristic curve*.

An image on video, when being recorded or edited, has the ability to change if the video or pedestal levels are altered, thus affecting the shot's gamma, or contrast range. So, this angle, which is basically fixed in a film stock, can be a variable in video.

gang

🎥 A cylinder with teeth inside a film synchronizer. Each gang keeps one audio or picture track in sync with the other gangs inside the synchronizer. Multiple gangs are used when editing in a tabletop situation, often in audio editing where multiple tracks are being built for the dubbing sessions, or in a negative cutting situation.

⇐ The video comparison would be a computerized editing system that ensures sync among multiple video playbacks or, in the audio situation, the multitrack that keeps up to 24 tracks of audio in sync with each other.

gate

🎥 An opening in a camera or projector, behind the lens and shutter, in which the film is held while being projected or exposed (Figure 25).

⇐ The area within a videotape machine where the videotape crosses the record or playback head.

🎥 **gauge** Format of a film as indicated by its width in millimeters. See also *formats*.

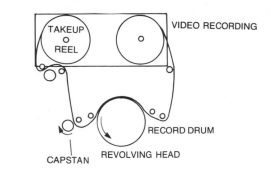

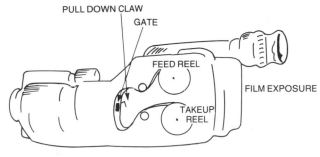

Figure 25 Capstan and camera. Although the camera pulls down and then exposes one frame at a time in an intermittent motion, videotape runs past revolving video heads at a constant speed.

gel   Short for gelatin. See also *gelatin.*

gelatin

Colored, heat-resistant material placed in front of lights to alter the color quality of the light; often called a gel or a filter.

The suspension medium in which silver halides are placed to create a film's emulsion.

The oxide particles comprising videotape are integrated with a carrier material called a binder, an equivalent to gelatin.

generation   The number of duplications away from the camera original. First generation would be one copy away from the original camera image.

generator lock   Also known as **genlock.**

Synchronizing an electronic machine with an incoming or prerecorded video signal to maintain complete synchronization with the rest of the electronic system. This concept is used extensively in video facilities where there are many pieces of equipment that have to be in electronic time with each other.

Although there is no house synchronizing signal in a film lab, there are voltage regulators on most of the lab's equipment that attempt to stabilize the power company's incoming voltage. Additionally, a system like Pilotone synchronizes different components of a film.

genlock   See *generator lock.*

gimbal   A mechanism that allows the camera to stay level even when the bottom of the device is tilted or moving. A gimbal is often used for effects such as a rocking ship, or other in-camera motion effects.

glitch   Any short interruption of a video signal. A glitch could be caused by bad tape stock, a poor edit, or a broadcast transmission problem.

grading

Timing a film; adjusting the color of each shot. See *timing.*

See *color correction.*

grain

The small globules of silver halide within a film emulsion that are exposed to light and create the image on film. These globules usually appear as an almost unnoticeable pattern of irregular shapes. In some cases, these shapes become more apparent and can be seen when the film is projected. In order to obtain a usable image under low light, faster film is required that uses larger globules of silver, and the net result is more visible film grain. Generally speaking, coarse grain is more sensitive to light but is also more noticeable to the viewer.

In low light conditions, some video cameras are able to create pictures. The trade-off is an increase of video noise. This noise is very apparent in home video cameras shooting in extremely low light situations.

☐ **grain reduction**   The electronic processing of a film to video picture in order to remove visible grain in the video signal. There are several devices that attempt this with varying degrees of success. See also *image enhancement.*

graphics

🎬 Artwork or titles that are to be included in a production either as entities unto themselves or composited with other images.

🎥 Film graphics can come from an artist's drawing or an art card. The use of the graphic within the film determines how a graphic is treated. If it is a title background, it is shot full frame and then composited in the optical printer. High-contrast film of titles is shot to provide hold-out mattes during the optical printing.

☐ Video graphics can be created on a paint system, an animation graphics system, or from an artist's drawing. Graphics systems usually have a video output and often can quickly create a hold-out matte or high-contrast for compositing at a later date. A drawing would be shot with a video camera.

☐ **gray scale**   A test pattern with incremental steps of brightness from gray to white. The pattern is often arranged in a logarithmic progression. The scale is used to calibrate video recording and playback decks.

🎥 **green print**   A processed film that has excess humidity in the emulsion, which can create damage or unsteadiness when run through a projector.

🎬 **green room**   A specific room where performers wait before going on stage. Originally a theater term that has been adopted by both video and film personnel, especially in live TV shows with an audience.

🎬 **grid**   The metal supports hung from the ceiling in a studio from which lights are hung. The term comes from the crisscross design the supports usually create.

🎬 **grip**   Crew member, often a member of a union, responsible for moving camera-support equipment, such as the tripod, dolly, and any other large, bulky items, in and around the camera.

🎬 **guide track**

1. A temporary audio track for the purpose of presentation and/or as a guide for the professional narrator.

2. An audio track recorded during production and used for lip syncing in post-production. An example of this would be in a music video when performers lip sync to a prerecorded track. This track is a guide, but not the properly mixed track that will be in the program.

halation

　Undesirable exposure that surrounds an overexposed (bright) image, caused by the emulsion near the image being exposed by light reflected from the film base or scattered within the emulsion. On most film stocks, there is a layer of antihalation material designed to prevent reflection during film exposure. See also *back coating*.

　When videotape is overexposed, the image is distorted during the recording process, and, as a result, tearing can occur. This is more likely to occur on location shoots and at night with cars' taillights in the frame. If the video is pushed or the camera lens fully opened, tearing may occur on the overexposed taillight.

half track　An audiotape recording with two tracks on quarter-inch tape. The difference between half track and stereo recording is that the recording surface areas of the former are narrower and the guard band between the recordings is wider, better eliminating cross talk.

hazeltine

　Manufacturer's name for a film electronic timing device, a color analyzer. Light is shone through the film, picked up by a video tube, then color reversed (if necessary), and finally displayed on a video screen. The CRT shows what the picture would look like if certain color changes were made during the printing process. The device prints a computer log of the different light values required for each scene, which will be loaded into the printer for use during the duping process. See also *color analyzer; color correction; timing*.

　Videotape can be and is color corrected but usually not to the extent that film is. There are varying degrees of color correction; however, most color adjustments are made within a telecine as part of the film-to-tape process. Reasons for this are that video cameras have the ability to electronically balance for most lighting conditions and video color and that lighting is not used as dramatically in video as it is in film.

HDTV   See *high definition television.*

head

1. In magnetic recording such as video and audio, an electromagnetic device that converts magnetic signals to electrical signals and vice versa. Electrical signals representing a video image or a sound pass through the head, which creates in the ferrous oxide of video- or audiotape a representative magnetic pattern. In playback, the head reads the magnetic pattern stored on tape and converts it back to electrical signals.
2. The top of a tripod (Figure 26). The head connects the camera and tripod.
3. The beginning of a segment, reel, or roll of videotape or film.

head clog

Buildup on the heads of small amounts of oxide from the videotape that crosses the heads. If the heads are not cleaned, they can lose their ability to read or record video information. Cleaning the heads with a specially made cloth and evaporative cleaner will usually eliminate the problem.

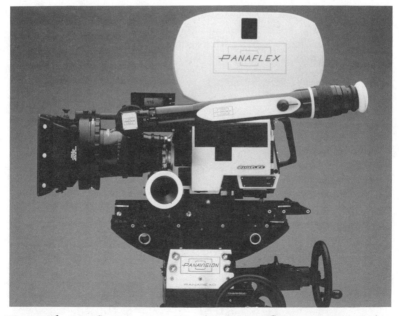

Figure 26   Panaflex camera and Panahead. A Panaflex camera mounted on a Panahead. Also note the white magazine atop the camera, the eyepiece just below the magazine, and the matte box that is mounted in front of the lens. Photo courtesy of the Panavision Corporation, Hollywood, CA.

↩ The comparative situation in film would be dust and/or hair in the camera or projector gate. Although the visual results will be different in appearance, the similarity is that of a foreign object blocking the ability to project or record a clear image.

headroom   The space, on screen, between a performer's head and the top of the screen. Because the film and video image is cropped during projection and broadcast, headroom should always be watched during shooting. Unless a shot is an extreme close up, inadequate headroom results in the appearance of a performer's head being chopped off.

helical scan   A method of recording a video signal diagonally across the width of a videotape. In this way, more of the tape is available for recording. Almost all video formats, with the exception of two-inch, use a helical scan recording method.

Hi8™

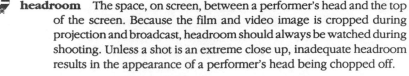

☐ A Sony Corporation trademarked name for their 8-millimeter wide video format that uses metal tape and is of higher quality than regular 8-millimeter.

↩ Super 16 film is to Hi8 as 16-millimeter film is to 8-millimeter; an improvement over an existing format, but not totally replacing it.

hi-con (high-con)   A black-and-white image that is made on high-contrast film and that is used in effects creation. The purpose of the hi-con is to stop video or light from reaching the record tape or film stock. The hi-con, then, is creating a hole, which is filled with picture. See also *effects*; *matte*.

high band

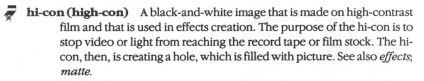

☐ Videotape recording process that produces a high quality picture using between 7.1 and 10 MHz for a recording frequency. One-inch, Betacam, three-quarter-inch, BVU, and digital video are high-band recording formats.

↩ The best comparison would be to 16- or 35-millimeter production footage. Low-band video recording would be similar to 8-millimeter or super 8 film.

high definition television (HDTV)

☐ A wide-screen, high-resolution television system that is the next generation of television broadcasting. Several high definition television systems are being examined by the Federal Communications Commission to be adopted in the United States. Japan already has an existing HDTV system, but domestic technical considerations are being examined before a U.S. standard is accepted. The U.S. standard video frame of the National Television Standards Committee (NTSC) is composed of 525 lines of information. The Phase Alternate Line (PAL) standard, used by many countries worldwide, including the United Kingdom, has a

625-line video frame. Proposed high definition television systems range from approximately 1000 to 1300 lines per frame. See also *scanning.*

By increasing the number of video lines, more detail is gained in the picture signal. Basically the television industry is reacting to dropping audience ratings in the same manner that the film industry did. When television threatened the film business, it responded by widening the screen, increasing the resolution of the image, and improving the sound quality of its product.

In the early years of film, the Academy aspect ratio was an acceptable standard of 1.33:1, the same ratio as television today. HDTV will increase the horizontal ratio (to around 1.78:1) and, in addition, the vertical resolution will be increased at least twofold. Just as the film industry enlarged its scope, television is following the same evolutionary path.

Hi-Vision

Trade name of the Japanese high definition television system being employed in that country. It has 1125 lines of information, 60 fields per second, with an aspect ratio of 16:9 (1.78:1). It remains to be seen if this particular system will be adopted by the United States' broadcast regulatory agency, the Federal Communications Commission.

Film's widening aspect ratios are the comparative aspect here. The several HDTV formats that will exist in the late 1990s would be the equivalent to the wide-screen ratios, 70-millimeter, Vista Vision, and even Cinemascope formats of feature film production.

hold

A designation by the director, with input from the production crew, to not print a take but not to file it away because it still may be used. Other common director designations are *print*, to make a positive copy and send it on to the editor, or *NG*, meaning *no good.*

The video director may give notes to the production assistant as to which version of a scene to use in post-production. These notes are often written on a script and sent to the editor or assistant director. However, all recorded takes are usually available to the video editor.

hold-out matte   A high-contrast, black-and-white image that is used in creating opticals and video effects. With film, the hold-out matte is used to mask film from being exposed in the optical printer. In video, the hold-out matte is fed to either the switcher or another effects device and used to electronically cut the hole in the background. See also *hi-con; key; matte.*

honey wagon   Trailers providing portable bathrooms and dressing rooms on sets and locations.

hook   See *skew.*

house sync

☐ A continuous signal created by a sync generator. This signal is a timing guide for all video devices that are within that system. Each device is electronically adjusted so that its signals are delivered in the same electronic timing as all the others. See also *generator lock*.

⇌ Although there is no house synchronizing signal in a film lab, there are voltage regulators on most of the lab's equipment in an attempt to stabilize the power company's incoming voltage.

houselights General illumination on a stage or set, not intended for production use.

hue

A specific wavelength range in the color spectrum; predominant color attribute.

☐ A control function of a time base corrector that adjusts the complete color spectrum either to the red or to the green. On a television set, it would be called tint.

⇌ Color control in film post-production occurs during the timing of the print. The film timing process has more control of the color values than the color correction of the video signal. See also *timing*.

IATSE Abbreviation for *International Alliance of Theatrical and Stage Employees*; a union of stage, film, and television workers.

IBEW Abbreviation for *International Brotherhood of Electrical Workers*, a union of public and private television employees.

image enhancement A process that sharpens the edges within a video picture and raises the apparent resolution of the image.

Image enhancers can be used at the tail end of a film-to-tape transfer system or in a video on-line editing system. Often, image enhancers are combined with noise reducers to counter the signal degradation caused by noise reduction. See also *grain; noise reduction.*

Imax A wide-screen format that is 70 millimeters wide and is projected onto especially designed screens. The newest improvement on this format, Imax Solido™, has a bowl-shaped screen. Audiences wear goggles with lenses incorporating liquid crystal shutters that alternately open and close electronically, giving the viewer a three-dimensional experience.

impedance A microphone's resistance to electrical flow. Generally speaking, the lower the impedance the better the microphone.

IN See *internegative.*

in house Company-owned equipment or facility (as opposed to an outside service company that would have to be paid).

in point The first frame of an edit.

in sync A situation in which picture and audio are matched precisely.

in the can A totally finished project, both aurally and visually. The concept comes from having a completed filmed show in a film can, ready for projection. The term has been embraced by the video world.

incidence exposure meter   An instrument that measures the intensity of light directed at an object. See also *CdS meter, exposure meter.*

industrial   A program that is designed for use internally within a company or as a company's business-to-business or business-to-consumer communication; a show that is not intended for broadcast.

in-frame edit   See *match frame.*

insert edit
A close shot, often using footage shot at a different time from principal photography.
An edit that falls between two other edits.

insert recording
A technical method of recording separately the functions of picture and sound; not to be confused with insert editing. (The alternative would be assembly recording, which erases and replaces audio, picture, and control track.) Insert editing does not disturb the tape's control track. Video-only and audio-only edits are possible when using insert recording.

In order for an insert recording to work, an assembly recording must have been performed on the videotape *prior* to the insert edit. Usually a whole reel of tape is prepared using an assembly recording (called edit black, video black, or black) before insert recording is begun.

A conceptual comparison to insert editing would be a tape splice of only the picture or audio track. The insert edit is not as creatively limited as the assembly edit. However, insert editing is, in a practical sense, used for work-print (off-line) or conforming (on-line) sessions.

inset
A smaller image picture placed within a larger one, created as an optical.
In video, the inset usually is created by a digital video effect device, like the rectangle over a newscaster's shoulder.

insurance shot   A protection shot.

INT.   Common script abbreviation for *interior.*

integration   To combine all elements for a show (commercials, promotions, programming, etc.).

interchangeable lens
Lenses of different, usually fixed focal lengths that fit into the same camera mount and work with the same camera.
Most video cameras have zoom lenses rather than fixed lenses.

interior   A simulated or actual inside of a building.

interlace   The scanning of a television frame by first scanning the odd-numbered lines, then the even-numbered lines. The two scans, each a field, comprise a single video frame. See also *scanning.*

☐ **interleaving** The combination of a color with a black-and-white signal. This process is used in the United States' domestic broadcasting system.

interlock

🎥 Running sound and picture together through a projector, when the two elements are on physically different playback materials. This often occurs during picture edits when one wants to screen the unfinished project. Since the audio is on mag film and picture is separate from this track, an interlock projector is used to view both, in sync on a screen.

➡ The video equivalent would be playing back a picture from a video source and the sound from a separate yet synchronous audiotape machine. This can occur in an editing bay using a multitrack audiotape recorder (ATR) or, more commonly, at a sweetening facility running a videotape machine slaved to the twenty-four-track machine.

intermittent

🎥 The motion of film traveling through the gate of a camera or projector. The film is pulled from the supply reel, held for a moment to either be projected or exposed, and then pulled out of the way to allow the next frame to be placed in the gate.

➡ Videotape travels continuously across the read or record heads at a constant speed, without stopping. Each format has its own speed unique to itself.

internegative (IN)

🎥 A negative film created from the interpositive (IP). In most cases, the internegative is duped from a timed (graded) IP. The internegative, or dupe negative, is often used to create positive prints for distribution or used in certain circumstances in the printing process. The internegative is a negative copy of the camera original, or film master, and is subsequently used for creating more copies.

➡ The video comparison to an internegative would be a dubbing master. The dubbing master, usually a protection copy of the edited master, is used to make broadcast copies of a program. In other cases, producers use the edited master as the dubbing master. For protection, a copy is made as soon as the edited master is approved.

interpositive (IP)

🎥 A positive film created from the original camera negative. The IP is either used as a protection for the cut negative or as an intermediate step in the process of making a print for projection. When the IP for printing is created, it is timed (color corrected). In the next pass through the printer, the timed IP produces a timed internegative. Prints for theatrical release are created from the internegative.

➡ The video image does not go through the lab process that film does. Certainly a broadcast program is dubbed a series of times, but the fact that video is a positive-to-positive process eliminates several post-production steps in comparison to film. Also, a generation of video is far less apparent than a generation of film.

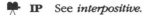

IP   See *interpositive*.

IPS   Abbreviation for *inches per second*, that is, the speed at which a tape moves across recording heads (audio or video). Although the IPS of a video machine is set by the manufacturer, tape is usually not referred to in inches per second but in program running time. In contrast, audio has several standard operating speeds that are commonly referred to; 7 1/2 IPS and 15 IPS are the two most widely used professional speeds.

iris   The lens opening that controls the amount of light entering a camera. See also *aperture; diaphragm; F-stop*.

iron cross   Also called a **Maltese cross**. Part of a gearing device that allows for the intermittent movement within a film projector or camera.

ISO   See *isolated camera*.

isolated camera (ISO)

A camera whose output is recorded on a tape machine separate from the line feed or switcher feed in a multicamera shoot. Some video productions isolate all camera outputs.

Every film camera is an isolated camera, as each camera's image is recorded separately from another's.

jam sync

- [ ] The process of locking a time code generator to a videotape, then recording that generator's code back onto that original tape or onto another tape. This is used to continue interrupted or terminated time code on a tape or to replace erased time code. See also *slaved time code*.
- ⟸ The film equivalent would be coding reprinted film or mag footage with the same markings as the original.

jenny A portable electric generator.

jib The projecting arm of a camera crane.

jog To move a picture slowly frame by frame.

joystick

- [ ] A device used to select source machines and to control playback speeds of tape machines.
- ⟸ A similar idea in film would be the foot controls found in different editing systems that drive the film mechanisms.

jump cut The seeming jump of aspects of a picture when two similar angles are cut together. A cutaway is often used to establish a comprehensible transition between these two similar shots. Occasionally a series of jump cuts is used as an effect.

Kem™ A registered trademark of a popular and often requested flatbed editing system (Figure 27). See also *flatbed*.

Kem rolls The term used for any picture and track prepared for use on a Kem or other flatbed editing system.

key numbers
A film stock identification system consisting of sequential combinations of numbers and letters appearing regularly on the edge of film. Key numbers are generally used for matching film negative and locating scenes. They are created by the film manufacturer, unlike code numbers, which are applied by post-production staff to work prints for internal editing purposes. Recent advances have brought the key number into the computer age. Kodak has encoded this information into a bar code (like those used in supermarkets) called KEYKODE™ (Figure 28). See also *code numbers; edge numbers*.

Video time code is the equivalent to key numbers in the video world. There are computer programs that can cross-reference time code and key numbers when electronic editing is used for film post-production. These conversions are used to provide a key list for negative cutting.

keying
The action of listing the key numbers so that the proper negative can be pulled for negative cutting. Usually the negative cutter does the keying.

The process of list cleaning the video edit decision list (EDL) is a comparison to the listing of the film key number. List cleaning usually employs a computer to eliminate edit overlaps.

The process of electronically cutting a hole in background video and inserting a picture, words, or color in that hole. Titles and graphics are usually keyed over scenes. A key filled in with a switcher-generated color is called a matte. A hold-out matte is used to create the pattern of an external key cut, which is filled with video from another source called the foreground.

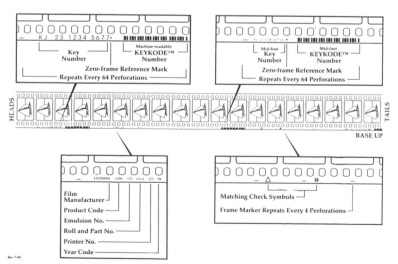

Figure 27 KEM eight plate flatbed. The flatbed editor can be in several configurations. This particular editor has three picture read heads. Note the speaker to the right of the center monitor. Also, adjustments can be made to replace picture with sound heads, allowing for multiple audio-track monitoring. Photo courtesy of KEM Picture Sound, Inc.

Figure 28 Eastman Keykode. The key number has its own code, indicating the critical elements of the film's manufacturing history as well as synchronizing marks used in matching negative to work print. Courtesy of Eastman Kodak Company.

➡ This process would equate to a stationary or traveling matte, used for compositing title cards and background images. In film, art cards are shot along with hold-out mattes. Then, the filmed art cards and background footage are married in the optical printer.

KEYKODE™

🎥 Eastman Kodak's machine readable bar code, created to enable computerized identification and tracking of film segments.

➡ This bar code is still a key number. The equivalent would be time code, the video frame-numbering system.

kines   See *Kinescope*.

Kinescope   Also called **kines** (pronounced ki-neees). A film image made by photographing a television monitor.

L cut A sync sound edit in which either the picture or sound precedes the other. See also *split edit.*

laboratory

The facility where exposed film is processed, producing an image on the film. This process takes place in highly controlled baths of solution through which the film is run. A string of film is run through these solutions, then dried to produce a developed image. Often, specific instructions are given to the laboratory in order to change the look of the film. The developing solution may be altered, as well as the speed at which the film is run through the solution, to compensate for conditions that existed during the production. See also *forced development; overexpose.*

The video equivalent of the laboratory is the decoding of the video signal after the recorded signal is read from videotape and displayed on a monitor. In a video recording, the video signal is modulated to a radio frequency for storage on tape. When the tape is played back, the encoded signal is read from the tape, then converted back to a video signal.

layback

The audio process of recording a final mix onto an edited videotape master. Usually this is accomplished by replaying the four elements (dialogue, narration, effects, and music) and recording them onto the edited master.

The film equivalent is the process of sending the audio from the final mixed tracks on film mag into a sound camera exposing the optical sound negative.

laydown

The recording of a telecine output onto a videotape.

The physical act of placing audio onto the multitrack for later mixing (sweetening).

103

⇒ The transferring of quarter-inch audio sources (effects, production sound, etc.) to film mag and editing them into a string in sync with the work print.

layering

▢ A video term that refers to making many recordings, adding effects, using a digital disk recorder, or digital videotape editing. Since editing in the digital domain means little signal loss, generation after generation of recordings can be made. One edit is made on a digital tape or side of a digital disk recorder, and then that master is played back and recorded onto another digital tape or the other side of a digital disk recorder (DDR). Adding a new element with each recording, the composite picture is bounced back and forth until the desired number of effects are achieved.

⇒ A film equivalent is the making of multiple passes within an optical printer. Each effect layered in a video suite could be compared to an effect created in an optical printer. As in video, it often takes several passes to properly execute an involved complicated effect in film.

leader

🎥 Blank film, often colored either white or black, used to maintain sync in A/B roll editing or to slug small amounts of the program where the trim (footage) is missing, or placed at the front of a reel or film segment. See also *fill; slug.*

📹 Blank film or tape used for various purposes. This is material specifically designed to be used in threading or for tailing out of the needed program material.

In film, white leader indicates the head of the reel. Black leader indicates the tail. The purpose of this leader is to protect the actual program from damage in the threading or unthreading process.

In a videotape cassette, the leader is usually a clear plastic, allowing light sensors to detect the beginning or end of the cassette's tape and, thus, to avoid ripping the tape off the end of the cassette.

📹 **lens**   A transparent piece of ground glass whose purpose is to focus a beam of light. In film, there are lenses in the camera as well as the projector, focusing light rays onto or from the film. Since there is no lens in a television set, the equivalent would be the red, green, and blue electron guns, the devices that shoot rays at the face of the television tube.

In wide-screen projection television, there are usually three lenses, one each for the red, green, and blue projectors.

📹 **lens shade**   A shield for the front of the lens to protect it from unwanted or direct light.

📹 **light box**   A box in which there is a light that shines through the translucent top of the box. A light box is for viewing or photographing slides or individual frames of film.

lighting   The illumination of a scene for film or video. Lighting will determine how that image is recorded. There are a series of terms specifically designed around lighting situations in these mediums. For the sake of simplicity, these terms have been listed in this section, rather than having individual entries.

LIGHTING INSTRUMENTS
(in order of power)

Inkie—small fresnel light, usually 100 watts.

Baby—A 750-watt incandescent light.

Seven-Fifty—a 750-watt incandescent light.

Ace—a 1000 watt incandescent light.

Deuce—a 2000-watt incandescent light.

Junior—a 2000-watt fresnel light.

Blonde—a 2000-watt variable-beam spotlight.

Brute—a 10,000-watt arc light.

Arc—a light designed to provide a high intensity of light by using an electron current that passes from one electrode to another; now being replaced by HMIs. The color temperature of an arc is close to that of daylight.

HMI—(halogen-metal iodide) a high-intensity light that uses a ballast, a device that regulates current passing through the fixture (Figure 29). Similar to a strobe operating at a high frequency, this type of light puts out a high-intensity, consistent light with a comparatively low heat

Figure 29   HMIs on location. On this location shoot, a crew is preparing for a shot. Two HIMs are seen, one on the left and one on the right. Note the scrims and flags used to control the light. Photo by Sean Sterling.

output. More efficient than quartz lights, they actually act like strobes, shutting off for part of a second to prevent massive heat build-up.

OTHER LIGHTING TERMS

Backlight—light coming from behind the subject. This type of lighting separates the subject from the background.

Barn doors—adjustable shades that frame a light; used to narrow or widen the light beam's coverage.

Bounce light—reflected light.

Cookie—opaque shapes designed to make specific patterns from shadows to be used in lighting a scene.

Incandescent light—the light resulting from a bulb that glows as a result of being heated.

Fill light—light cast on shadow areas to reduce contrast.

Flag—an adjustable, rectangular card or other material mounted on a stand and positioned between a light source and object to create shadows or to block light.

Flood lights—lights that evenly illuminate a large area.

Fresnel lens—a lens with a stepped shape. Where most lights need a lens or curved backing to reflect the light, this unique lens focuses the light rays without a heavy concave lens. The fresnel light is often used as a key light.

Gobo—precut blockers to make or control shadows.

Gel—a filter placed in front of a light to change the color of that light.

Kelvin—a measure of color temperature, often abbreviated *K* but described in degrees.

Key light—the primary source of illumination. This is a hard light source, also usually creating the primary shadows of the scene.

Kick—unwanted light reflection.

Kicker—a light that provides additional backlight.

Lighting ratio—the ratio of key light added to the amount of fill light, compared to the fill light alone.

Lumen—a measure of light; equal to one foot candle of light covering one square foot.

Net—a camera filter manufactured from a netlike material that softens the focus of a shot and also reduces the color saturation of that shot.

Neutral density filter—a camera filter that reduces the light levels that reach the lens without altering the color values of the light.

Quartz lamp—a lamp with a tungsten filament enclosed in a quartz housing, used for set illumination; also known as a quartz halogen lamp.

Reflectors—materials used to bounce sunlight onto a subject.

Rim light—a back light that creates a halo effect.

Scrims—wire meshes mounted on the light in order to reduce light intensity. Scrims usually reduce light equal to one full stop.

Spotlight—a light with a focused beam designed to illuminate a specific area.

Spot meter—a device designed to measure a level of light in a small area.
Strip—a length of lights.
Xenon—a lamp or light containing xenon gas.

limiter   An audio device that acts as a gate, not allowing sounds above a predetermined level to pass through; similar to a processing amplifier or clipping circuitry in a video system.

linear editing

☐ The normal method of video editing, recording each edit, one after another, onto a videotape.

Since linear editing is an actual, physical recording, any change in an edit's length would then require that each subsequent edit be rerecorded to reflect this change in the program.

The easiest method of solving this problem quickly is playing back the edited master onto another tape. This way a new edited master is created, thus eliminating the need to rerecord every edit. Unfortunately, this may result in an extra generation of video copying and significantly eroded image quality in analog (nondigital) video formats.

⟸ The conceptual equivalent to linear editing would be the film process of making an answer print. If a print is struck and needs a shot change, then the print has to be struck again.

lip sync   The technical coordination of a character's voice and apparent lip motion.

In film, when using production sound, this is a matter of keeping the image of the clapsticks (slate) at the scene beginning in sync with the sound, and then keeping the relative sync together.

In video, when using production sound, it is a matter of matching time code numbers.

There are many instances, though, where the production sound is not used. In these cases, lip sync becomes especially critical because the words spoken were not spoken at the same time the visuals were made. Some instances of this would be:

1. Pretending to sing to a prerecorded audio track, as in a music video or musical production.
2. When a director likes a particular shot visually, but chooses a read (dialogue) from another take.
3. A dialogue replacement that is recorded on a dubbing stage (ADR) and then added to the program.
4. Split edits, where audio from one shot leads the picture of that shot; for instance, cutting from a close-up to a two shot. The audio from the two shot might be put into lip sync with the close-up.

liquid gate

🎥 A device that contains a continuously filtered liquid (usually perchlorethylene) through which film passes during a printing process. By immersing film during the printing process, the liquid fills in the scratches and reduces the visibility of the damage to the film (depending on the size of the scratch). Liquid gate printers are found on certain contact printers and some optical printers.

⇌ The dropout compensator (DOC) is a comparative piece of equipment to the liquid gate. The DOC, usually located inside or connected to a VTR, senses the lack of oxide on a tape and compensates for the missing visual information.

list cleaning

☐ The process of eliminating all unneeded edits in the edit decision list (EDL) before on-lining (conforming) the program. During the editing process, many edits and portions of edits are erased as creative decisions are made, thus producing inconsistencies and missing information. The cleaning can be done manually but usually is accomplished by a computer.

⇌ Since the work print delivered to the negative cutter for conforming should not include any extraneous material, there is no comparison for a list cleaning process.

location   Any production locale that is not situated on a film or television studio site. Shooting at a studio but not actually in the studio is often called the backlot.

locked   Term originating from film indicating that the creative picture process is over and has been approved. From here, audio dubbing and other post-production processes can proceed at full speed.

lock-off   A production term referring to a shot in which the camera is not moved and is secured in its spot. This type of condition occurs when effects that are to be created will be using production footage. The stationary shot makes the post-production process much easier.

lock-up time

📹 The time it takes a synchronizing device to lock to its source. This could indicate a film camera getting up to regular operating speed, dummies ramping up to full sound speed, or the time any other device requires to reach its required operating speed in sync.

☐ The term has the same use in video. Another term often used is *preroll*, the time it takes to synchronize video or audio devices prior to actual recording.

logs

📹 A record containing information about various aspects of the film production and/or post-production stages. There are several types of logs created during the run of a filmed project. The first log created is the *continuity log*. This report, made by the script supervisor or continuity assistant, notes changes in the script, director's comments, and alterations in the original production plan. These are extremely helpful when the editor begins cutting the film.

The second log is the *camera report*, the camera department's record of what happened during production, what type of film is being used, the weather conditions, under- or overexposure, and so forth. The camera report also indicates if a specific type of effect is being attempted. Most feature film productions only print selected scenes. The camera log will note which scenes were to be printed and the reasons why the others were not printed.

The *sound log* accompanies the camera log and is basically the same concept as the camera report, except the log originates from the sound department. Takes that are used, ambient sound recording, and other descriptions of the sound recordings are made. As with the camera department, not all the sound is transferred to magnetic film. So, the sound log describes all the available sound and whether it had problems during production.

Logging of the production-footage edge numbers is another important part of record keeping. As each shipment of footage is received in the editing room from the lab, the edge numbers at the head and tail of the shot are logged in a *code book*. In this way, there is an accurate listing of edge numbers from all the footage printed.

There may well be a continuity log from a video production. However, usually the production assistant's *marked script* fulfills this purpose. In a multicamera shoot, such as a sitcom, lines are drawn down the script with shot descriptions and time code written in the margins. Director's notes and comments are also noted.

In a documentary situation, a *master footage log* is often created. Once the original footage is duplicated on window dubs, the footage is logged in a large notebook, with time code, reels, and comments. This type of log is also created for long video projects. Some producers load this information into a computer data base for easy access to reels and time code numbers. Because sitcoms are usually shot in script order, there is little need for a master log. Carefully marked scripts are used for footage reference.

longitudinal time code (LTC)

Time code that is recorded on an audio track. This type of recording is a digitally encoded audio signal and can only be read when the film or tape is in motion. Time code is used in many situations: video editing, some random-access film editing, and 24-track sweetening. Alternative time-code recording methods are address track and vertical interval.

The general comparison to time code is key numbers, the marking of film frames on the edge of film. See also *address track time code; time code; vertical interval time code.*

loop

Also known as **film loop**. A section of film spliced head to tail, making an endless piece that repeats itself on playback. The loop may be of picture or sound. Loops are used at point-of-purchase displays and in automatic dialogue replacement (ADR) sessions.

⟶ Video is usually not spliced together in a loop. Instead, in the case of ADR, the videotape is computerized and rewound for each read. In point-of-purchase displays, the videotape machine can be programed to rewind and play again. In this situation, usually the program is repeated a number of times over the length of the tape.

looping See *automatic dialogue replacement*.

low band

☐ Low frequency recording, such as used in VHS and Betamax recordings. Broadcast formats use higher frequencies and are called high band recordings.

⟶ The best film comparison to low band would be 8-millimeter production footage. High band video recording would be similar to 16- or 35-millimeter footage.

☐ **LTC** See *longitudinal time code*.

lumen A measurement of light equal to one foot candle covering one square foot. See also *foot candle; lighting*.

☐ **luminance** The amount of pure white in a picture signal. The FCC has defined the technical limits of all aspects of the video signal, including luminance. In terms of luminance, the IRE (a standard) measured levels for over-the-airwaves broadcasting should not be below 7.5 percent or over 105 percent in white value.

☐ **luminance signal** In component video, the signal determining the brightness of an image, as opposed to its color. The luminance signal is skimmed in calculated proportions from signals produced by the three color CCDs or pickup tubes. These color-brightness proportions composing the luminance signal are approximately 30 percent red, 59 percent green, and 11 percent blue. The luminance signal is also sometimes referred to as the Y channel.

MII™   Panasonic's half-inch broadcast video format whose major competitor is Sony's half-inch Betacam format. See also *formats*.

m and e track(s)   Single or multiple audio tracks with just music and effects (containing no dialogue or narration). These tracks are often used to create foreign releases or in various advertising campaigns, as well as for archival purposes. With dialogue and narration stripped from the program's audio, new narration or foreign-language dialogue can be combined to produce a quality foreign release.

mag   See *magnetic film*.

magnetic film   Also called **mag.**
   Audiotape with sprocket holes and the same size as production film. Magnetic film, usually called mag or full coat, is used in the editing process to cut audio. The quarter-inch original-production audio recording is transferred to mag, thus allowing the editor to splice the soundtrack(s) in the same manner as the picture. See also *full coat; single-stripe film; three-stripe film*.
   Videotape equivalent would be a multitrack audiotape. Multitrack tape can have up to 24 tracks of available audio track space, depending on the equipment used. Multitrack audio processing does not physically cut tracks as you would with mag, but transfers from one track to another, or bounces from the multitrack to an outside source (another multitrack quarter-inch tape, digital audio workstation, etc.) and then back.

magnetic head   In audio and video and other magnetic recording mediums, an electromagnetic device that converts magnetic signals to electrical signals and vice versa. See also *head* (1).

maltese cross   See *iron cross*.

master log book

A comprehensive, precise, and authoritative listing of production footage and its correlation to the script and other production elements. The master log book is designed to facilitate the locating of footage after the shooting. Some production companies and editors have begun to use computers to create and store their master logs. There are specific programs that are designed to function as master logs and that also can print trim tabs and labels. Other companies are modifying standard computer data base software to serve as master logs.

The master log book is created when dailies arrive at the editing room. All pertinent information is written into the master log. Some information comes from the film or clapstick: scene, take, date, key number. Some information comes from the camera report: camera roll, sound roll, and possible technical flaws. Some information comes from the continuity script: director's notes and production notes.

Key numbers are notated in the log book as the work print is broken down and audio is synchronized with picture. When the broken-down dailies return from coding, the code numbers are also written into the master log.

The master log in video is similar to the film master log, but its structure and form is far less formal than that of film. The video log contains all the necessary information to find a shot. The master log contains technical information, director's and production notes, and a fairly detailed shot description as well as the time code of each shot. In some cases, marked production scripts are used as a replacement for the master log.

match cut

Editing together two differently angled shots of the same or continuing event, ensuring for a viewer the appearance of uninterrupted action. The edit is selected so that a viewer finds the change in perspective smooth and not distracting.

An edit that precisely continues a previously edited scene. For example, if a long scene were copied to a record tape and the editor wished to continue the scene, he or she would match cut the continuing segment rather than recopying entirely the original scene plus the continuation. See also *match frame*.

match frame

An edit on the record tape, continuing where the last edit left off. It is sometimes referred to as a *match-frame edit* or an *in-frame edit* and is often used in building effects. The reason for such an edit is to reload playback tapes for a dissolve or other effect.

The film equivalent would be the footage count where in an optical printer a new effect is to begin.

matching action   A movement that is repeated in several camera angles and then edited so that the action seems to be in one continuous flow. See also *match cut, match frame.*

matte (post-production)

A device that is used to create a hole that, in film, is filled with another *picture* and in video, with a *color.*

A film matte is an effect created through the use of four different elements: the background, the foreground, and the two hold-out mattes. The actual matting process takes place inside an optical printer. Film titles utilize mattes, as do miniatures, split screens, and matte paintings.

1. A video matte is a hole that is electronically cut out of a background picture and that has a switcher-created color inserted into that hole. This is different in concept from the film matte and is used to colorize titles.

2. A hold-out matte is a **high-contrast image**, used like a film matte, to use in cutting the hole for a graphic or image.

matte (production)   A mask placed in front of the camera lens. Some productions use this effect during production rather than in post-production. Common matte shapes would be a keyhole or binocular shapes. The matte is placed in a holder in the matte box.

matte (projection)   When a format is enlarged for projection, it is usually made from a standard 35-millimeter-sized print; but the image also is expanded horizontally during the projection process. In order to eliminate the unwanted top and bottom of the horizontally expanded frame, a masking device called a matte is attached to the projector.

matte box

A device that is used to protect the lens from ambient light produced by or reflected from objects that are not part of the action. It can also hold a matte, a mask placed in front of the lens to block part of the action, or it can accept filters. The matte box can be of rigid or bellows design. The rigid design is somewhat limited in that it cannot be adjusted as different-sized lens are used. The adjustable matte box is more flexible as it can be folded back with shots employing wide-angle lens.

The video camera can also have a similar device, usually called a lens hood or lens shield. Its purpose is to limit the amount of ambient light striking the lens just as the film matte box does.

metal tape   See *chromium dioxide tape.*

mixer

1. An audio control board used to combine various sources of sound (Figure 30). There are many types of mixers, from simple

Figure 30 Neve audio console for music, film, and post-production. This type of console is used in production, as well as post-production, to control multiple audio sources. Note that the console is divided vertically. Each *column* is designed to control one source. These complicated devices have the capability to be computer assisted. Photo courtesy of the Neve Corporation.

devices to complicated, multi-input apparatus that is computer controlled.

2. A person who uses a mixing board.

➡ The film equivalent is the rerecordist, the person who runs the mixing board, combining all the sound elements.

mixing

☐ The combining of all the audio tracks into one or more tracks. The tracks being mixed could be one or all of the following: ADR, Foley, effects, dialogue, music, and/or production tracks.

First, the production tracks are transferred to a multitrack audio tape recorder (called a multitrack). At the same time, picture is copied onto a videotape, usually a three-quarter-inch tape. The process of transferring picture and sound is called a *lay down*. This copy is kept in sync with the multitrack so that the mixer can see the picture to which he or she is mixing.

A multitrack can have 4, 16, 24, 36, or 48 separate tracks available for recording or playback functions. On a dedicated track, time code is recorded from the source videotape. Placed on the other available tracks are effects, music, Foley sounds, narration, and other audio sources. Once all the audio sources have been placed, the four separate tracks, effects, music, dialogue, and narration, are each laid onto a separate track at the proper level and equalization.

When the mix has been approved, it is recorded onto the original videotape in a process called a *lay back*. Usually a protection copy of the final mixed (sweetened) tape is dubbed.

➡ The mixing process in film is called dubbing. In this process, a series of audio playback machines (called dubbers) are used, rather than the multitrack, and the final mix is recorded onto magnetic film (mag), rather than the multitrack. In film dubbing, the sound editor is responsible for arranging all the tracks of the audio.

mode

☐ **1.** The type of edit that is being performed by a video editing machine and indicated on a computerized edit decision list (EDL). The mode is either a dissolve, indicated by a *D*; a wipe, *W*; a cut, *C*; or a key, *K*. See also *edit decision list.*

➡ The film comparisons would be grease-pencil markings on the film indicating what type of effect is going to be used in the work print or the request sent to the optical house for a specific type of optical.

2. The method in which a videotape edit decision list (EDL) is implemented. There are a series of organizational designs to on-lining a video program. The modes, in ascending alphabetical order, become increasingly complicated. In preparing an EDL, computers are usually used to clean the EDL of unwanted edits and edits that have been recorded but subsequently altered in length by additional editing. Each mode is described below; however, many on-line sessions may include a variety of modes, depending on the EDL that is brought to the session and on the on-line editor.

A Mode. All the edits are recorded in sequential order. The first edit in the list is the first picture of the program. Reels are put up on playback machines as each edit requires them with no real regard as to how many times that particular reel is loaded.

B Mode. The list is organized by reel numbers. All edits from one reel are grouped together within the edit list, and each edit is listed in its show order within this grouping. In the on-line session, the clustered edits requiring the same source reel are completed together, even if their places within the final program are far apart. The source reel shuttles among appropriate source points, and the destination reel or reels are shuttled similarly as each edit in the cluster is performed. When the cluster is finished, the next source reel is loaded and the next cluster of edits is performed. See also *checkerboard assembly.*

C Mode. This is an enhancement of B Mode. In this assembly process, the edit decision list is organized by reel number as in B Mode, except the source points of edits are listed in ascending order. As a result, the record tape is constantly shuttling back and forth, but the playback just moves forward as each edit is performed.

D Mode. This is basically the same as B Mode, but with the edit list being organized by reel numbers. All edits from one reel are in one area of the edit list, and each edit is listed in its show order. The difference between B Mode and D Mode is that D Mode lists the effects at the end of the edit decision list.

E Mode. This is basically the same as C Mode, in that the edit decision list is organized by reel number and the edits are listed in ascending playback order. However, all effects are listed at the end of the edit decision list.

⮐ The negative cutting list is in order of shot appearance and is assembled on a reel in shot order. Basically, the film method of conforming negative is equal to an A Mode assembly.

modulation

☐ The alteration of an oscillation (a wave) to encode another signal onto that oscillation. The alteration can be to the amplitude (AM), the frequency (FM), pulse width, pulse code (PCM), or pulse position. This coding process is also used to record or broadcast audio signals as well as video.

⮐ The comparison to modulation in a broadcast transmission sense would be the transportation of the film print to the theater. In the recording situation, where the video is modulated, the comparative situation would be the developing of the film.

monitor

  1. The act of listening to or watching the creation of a program.

2. An audio speaker used to listen to sound.

3. Viewing device used to review a video-assist output.

☐ 1. An extremely high resolution **cathode ray tube** (CRT) used in important viewing areas. Usually a monitor does not have any audio capabilities, nor the ability to receive television broadcast signals. The monitor receives its signals from a video input rather than over the air waves. Recently there have been some consumer monitors being marketed that also have audio and broadcast reception capabilities.

2. On a camera, a viewfinder that allows the operator to view what the camera is photographing.

montage

1. Editing a quick-paced series of images together, often creating a story from the visuals and containing very little dialogue. The montage is often cut to the beat of a music track.

2. A brand name (Montage) of random-access video-editing machine.

MOS   An abbreviation indicating the shot is without sound. In the early days of film, there were several prominent directors who came from Germany.

The story goes that the Germans constantly said "mit out sound," which eventually was shortened to MOS.

muddy   Term meaning not clear in an audio sense or too dark in a picture sense.

multiplex   Using one channel or signal to carry several sources or signals. Examples would be broadcasting stereo sound over one channel or several television signals over a single cable.

multitrack   An audiotape with multiple tracks or audio tape recorder/ player capable of accessing multiple audio tracks. Multitracks are usually found in video sweetening facilities; however, there is a trend for film audio to be finished on multitrack systems.

Mylar™   A polyester film used as a base for magnetic tape. Mylar is the base of magnetic film (mag), quarter-inch audiotape as well as videotape. Mylar is a registered trademark of DuPont.

Nagra™

Brand name of a quarter-inch audio tape recorder/player used in film-production audio recording (Figure 31). These sophisticated tape recorders can record Pilotone and/or time code on the quarter-inch tape. See also *Pilotone; time code.*

☐ The Nagra is used to transfer film-production audio to videotape in transfer processes.

narrative The story of a show.

narrow gauge film

A film that is less than 35 millimeters wide. This would include super 16, 16-millimeter, super 8, and 8-millimeter film.

⇐ The comparison in video would be nonbroadcast formats (VHS, Betamax, 8 millimeter). Just as narrow-gauge film is used in some circumstances for feature film production, nonbroadcast tape formats are occasionally used for television production.

neg Abbreviation for *film negative.* See also *negative.*

negative

Film stock in which, when developed, the colors of the subject appear as their complementary (opposite) colors. Camera original film footage generally is negative stock.

⇐ The video comparison is videotape, the stock that stores picture information of the original scene.

negative cutting

The process of conforming camera original negative to the editor's fine-cut work print. Film negative is extremely sensitive to dust and dirt, and thus must be handled in laboratory conditions and as little as possible. In addition, negative splices are cement splices, rather than tape splices, and are permanent; so only trained, experienced technicians are hired to cut film negative.

Figure 31 Nagra audio recorder. Note the bridge of the three VU meters used to monitor sound levels just below the tape machine. Photo by Sean Sterling, courtesy Cinesound, Hollywood, CA.

To make a change after a cement splice is made, two frames are lost—one frame from the outgoing scene and one from the incoming scene. Therefore, special care must be made in keeping the film negative clean and in making the correct splice on the correct frame. See also *cement splice*.

➡ The video comparison to negative cutting is the final on-line session. There are other considerations, besides picture conforming, that take place in the video on-line: sync sound placement and/or mixing, color correction, and effects creation.

NG Notation for *no good*; indicates a rejected take.

ni-cad A rechargeable, portable battery.

noise

1. Unwanted sound on an *audio* track. Noise can have originated naturally during production location or studio recording, resulting from an uncontrollable noise source (called ambient noise) or technically from the actual recording medium (called system noise).

2. Undesirable visual material on a *video* track. There are several sources of video noise: shooting in low-light situations, chroma noise, and excessive film grain. Some video noise can be reduced through the use of a noise reduction device.

noise reduction
1. In audio, using a device designed to reduce any unwanted audio noise, which could be both ambience noise and system noise. An equalizer can increase or decrease specific audio frequencies. Ambient noise, like a hum from a machine, could be isolated and selectively eliminated. There are also devices to reduce audio noise inherent in the recording medium, specifically Dolby™ noise-reduction systems.
2. In video, using a device called a noise reducer to reduce any unwanted video noise. Some of the major sources of video noise are low-light-level production, chroma noise, and film grain.

non-drop frame time code
☐ A method of numbering, for identification and editing purposes, every video frame with a sequential, time-based code that is generally but not precisely consistent with actual clock time.

When time code was originally introduced, the time code (now called non-drop frame) ran at 30 frames per second. However, video is projected at 29.97 frames per second. For a short program, this error of 0.03 frames per second presents no problem. But over the span of an hour, this error translates to 3.6 seconds more time code than program. To alleviate this problem, drop frame time code was introduced. See also *drop frame time code*.

The film key numbers are similar to time code, being a numbering system that identifies individual frames of visual information. Key numbers are visible to the eye. Computerized code, like Keykode™, has to be decoded by a machine.

nonlinear In post-production, a system's ability to allow users to change any edit and not have to specifically alter other edits to accommodate the change. The system automatically changes the position (time code parameters) and other technical aspects of other edits in response to the initial change. Film editing is by nature nonlinear editing since, given that film segments are physically spliced together, individual segments can be accessed and altered with no resulting impact on subsequent segments.

Video nonlinear editing is accomplished through the use of sophisticated, computer-controlled editing machines. Some of these devices are based on videotape playback systems, some are based on video disk playback systems, and others can handle either.

The concept of video nonlinear editing is that sequences of edits are not actually recorded, only held in a system's memory and previewed. Being able to preview multiple edits requires multiple playback sources, or relatively expensive disk players (a copy of the video material has to be transferred temporarily to the video disk). This reality tends to make nonlinear editing systems somewhat expensive, compared to traditional video-editing systems.

☐ **NTSC**

1. Abbreviation indicating the technical color broadcast and video recording system used in the United States. This system defines video as having 525 interlaced scan lines per frame, a frame rate of approximately 30 frames per second, and a 60-hertz transmission standard.

2. Abbreviation for the National Television Standards Committee, the group originally responsible for determining the U.S. system of color broadcasting.

nut   The cost of a project's production.

off-line

An editing process that produces a rough cut; a work print during which most editing decisions are made. At its simplest, a show can be off-line edited using two home video decks to put together a rough idea of a program. At its peak, off-line would employ a sophisticated computer and several playback units to put together a polished work print and computerized listing of each edit. In the middle area are a variety of midrange video cassette controllers that will perform edits without costing a fortune to rent or purchase. Basically the video off-line process begins with a window dub of the original material.

The film editing work-print process is the equivalent of the video off-line process. The film is logged, assembled, and edited until the program is ready for negative cutting. The film work-print stage results in the same product as the off-line edit: a physical, viewable print that reflects the show's editorial decisions.

off-mike Recording an audio source at such a distance from the microphone that the sound is not full volume and appears to be at a distance. This effect is usually a negative aspect of sound recording but, on occasion, can be used as an audio effect.

omnidirectional microphone A microphone with a pickup pattern sensitivity that is the same in all directions from the microphone. See also *cardioid microphone, shotgun microphone.*

one light

A dupe, or copy, of camera original. The lab checks the footage to determine an acceptable average setting for color for the reel. Then a positive copy is made using this one color setting. The one light is used only for work print and viewing of dailies.

The video equivalent to a one-light print is a window dub. The window dub is an exact duplicate of the camera original, with time code recorded on the address track or on an audio channel, as well as in the picture.

☐ **on-line** The final editing process. The process of on-line editing is one of completion and may encompass one or more of the following aspects:
1. Placement of audio elements or, possibly, mixing for broadcast and/or presentation.
2. Placement of camera original footage, following an off-line work print. This may be an automated process of conforming an edit decision list, creating a segment or shot from a handwritten viewing list, eye matching footage from a work print, or any combination of these three examples.
3. Incorporation of effects/opticals; the creation of keys, mattes, dissolves, wipes, and digital effects.

With very complicated layering, a separate on-line session is often performed before the program on-line session.

Like film post-production, there are specific pieces of equipment that are used to create a final video product. Probably the biggest difference is that video effects can be created either during the show assembly or in a separate editing session. A show might use one video facility for effects and another for show assembly, or effects could be created during the conforming of the show to the work print. In either case, the edit session would be called an on-line because the results would be used in the final program. Some complicated effects are performed in paint/graphics systems. See also *graphics*.

EXPLANATION OF SOME VIDEO ON-LINE EFFECTS
All the following examples assume the existence of a record machine. See also *opticals*.

Dissolve—Requiring A and B reels on separate playback reels, it is a matter of programming the video switcher to perform a gradual transition from the A to the B source. If both sources are on the same reel, a dub is made of one of the scenes. See also *B reel*.

Fade—A fade to or from black is performed by the switcher. Only one source is required to fade to black unless there is a multiple-source effect being faded to or from black.

Flip—Flipping an image requires a DVE device, a switcher for compositing, and the source material.

Matte—A video matte is a key (hole cut in the background) filled with a color. The hole can come from a variety of sources: character generator, art card, DVE. The color fill is often from the switcher background-color generator.

Chroma key—The chroma key requires a switcher and two play-back sources, one with the background source and the other with the foreground (insert) image shot in front of a solid, flatly lit, colored backing. See also *B reel*.

Reverse action—This effect needs a source machine that is capable of variable-speed playback and dynamic tracking. Most tape machines with reverse action capability have a reverse-speed maximum one times sound speed and a forward-speed maximum of three times sound speed. A reverse-action effect faster than one times sound speed, thus, would require initially dubbing the tape going backwards and then recording it at a variable speed forward.

Faster than three times sound speed would require multiple recordings or the transferring of footage to a digital disk recorder (DDR) that has forward and reverse limits of 30 times sound speed.

Skip frame—There are several devices that can perform skip frames, an effect with a result like speeded motion and that is produced by printing or dubbing only frames selected at regular intervals. Some DVE devices can be programmed for skip frames. Simple skip frames can be accomplished through single-frame editing with a standard computer editor. Digital disk recorders can be programmed to create skip-frame effects.

Split screens—This is usually performed through the use of multiple DVE devices if picture has to be repositioned for the split. In that case, a switcher is used to combine the various DVE video outputs into one signal and to combine A and B source material.

If the footage has been shot in its proper position, all that is needed is a switcher and the A and B source reels.

Stop frame—This effect, also called a freeze frame, can be created in several devices: variable-speed video machines, digital video effects devices, digital disk recorders, and frame store devices. A source is needed to make the stop frame.

Titles—Titles can also come into being from several sources. First, the printed words can come from art cards, a videotape source, or a character generator. The art card is shot with an essentially standard camera. The switcher combines this camera output, a videotape source or character generator signal with a background source. If the tape, character generator, or camera is the only source, a switcher may not be needed.

Wipe—Requiring A and B reels on separate playback reels, creating the wipe is a matter of programming the video switcher to perform a particular design of wipe—with or without a border, hard or soft edged—to transition at a certain frame rate from the A source to the B source. Not all wipes are available on all switchers.

To create an unusual wipe, a high-contrast transition from black to white can be created; then, using the hi-con as a hold-out matte, the transition can be made using the switcher's keying circuitry. See also *B reel*.

Zoom—A zoom is created either in telecine or by using a digital video effects device to increase the size of the source material. Each

DVE device has varying limits as to what percentage an image can be increased without noticeable picture degradation.

opaque A material that will not transmit light.

open mike A microphone that is *live*, that is, whose sound is being either monitored or recorded, or both.

open reel A videotape format that is not enclosed. Two-inch (quad) and one-inch formats are open-reel formats. Three-quarter-inch, Betacam, and VHS formats are examples of cassette tape, that is, tape and reels that are enclosed in a protective plastic case.

optical multiplexer A system that has the ability to transfer slides and motion picture to videotape by aiming a projector directly into a video camera.

optical printer See *printer*.

optical sound
A method of sound recording and playback used in film prints. Optical sound is created by taking the final mix and printing onto a film negative edge stripe a continuously varying pattern of dye densities that is an analog of the sound track.

In the projector, the optical stripe passes under an exciter lamp. Above it is a sensor that detects the differences in light intensity and that in turn produces the sound. Optical sound is used in the final stage of the print process (not at all in the dubbing stage.).

In video production, sound either may be recorded on the picture videotape or on a separate recorder. The sound track is then mixed during post-production and ultimately laid back, that is, electronically transferred to the final edited master. Unlike film optical sound, all video sound is magnetically recorded and copied. See also *lay back*; *lay down*; *sweetening*.

opticals
Effects created in the optical laboratory. There are various forms of opticals and a variety of methods for achieving different types of opticals (Figure 32). Once the optical has been created and approved, it is edited into the program's negative by the negative cutter.

The following effects take advantage of the optical printer's varied lens configurations and ability to open and close the iris separating the source footage from unexposed raw stock: blow-ups, diffusion, dissolves, fades, flips (like a DVE flip), flopovers (reversing screen direction), reverse action, skip frame, split screen, stop frame (freeze), stretch frame, wipes, and zooms. See also *effects*; *graphics*; *on-line*.

Titles and mattes are created in a similar manner and are a little different than the opticals described above. Before the matte is at-

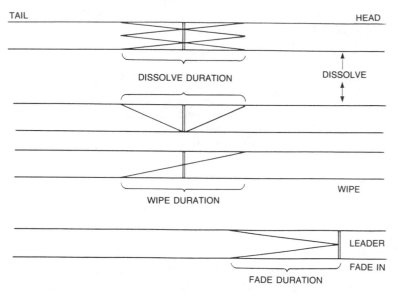

Figure 32 Optical effects markings. Film and video use similar effects, but the manner in which they are indicated to others in the field are vastly different. The video editor uses an edit decision list to convey edit information. The film editor uses visual marking on the work print.

tempted, hi-con elements are needed to prevent certain areas of the film from being exposed. Hi-cons are created by exposing high contrast film to the production footage through an optical printer. The hi-con is created on the same optical printer on which the effect will be composited so that all the physical aspects of the effect are consistent.

Once the hi-cons are developed, they are used to composite the footage, whether it is titles, other production footage, matte paintings, or miniature footage. With computer-controlled cameras, hi-cons can be created during production by the same camera that will be used to shoot the footage, repeating the shot a second time with high-contrast film.

The equivalent in video would be special effects. Some video special effects are performed in an on-line session or in a paint/graphics system. Other, extremely complicated compositing sessions can take place in a series of locations. These sessions can be specifically designed to create the special effect or included in the on-line of the complete program, depending on the complexity of the particular effect.

oscilloscope A CRT device designed to monitor variations in electrical quantities. The display is in the form of a continuously varying visible wave.

out of sync A condition in which picture is ahead or behind the sound track; a disjunction in timing. In film, this can occur if the picture is not properly synchronized with the separate sound track in the daily process or in the editing process. In the video domain, this can occur if an audio-only edit is performed improperly, throwing the track out of sync, or if the sweetening process lays back the audio in an improper place. Proper matching of picture and sound time code (in video, key numbers, and/or code numbers in film) ensures synchronization.

The most obvious example of being out of sync is in old television shows or movies that have been transferred to videotape through a frame store device. Copying video through this device delays the picture (but not the sound) one frame with each pass. Multiple passes ruin the audio sync. See also *frame store; lip sync.*

out take A take and/or angle that has been shot but not used in the final cut of the production.

overage A financial term indicating either the amount a production goes over its original budget or a bill for additional money.

overcrank

To speed up the film within the camera in order to create a slow-motion effect. Increasing the film speed means that more frames are exposed per unit of time than at normal film speed. Thus, when projected at normal film speed, an event is portrayed over a longer period of time—in slow motion. Either a filter or iris adjustment is used to compensate for the difference in light levels.

The video recorder runs at a constant speed. The shutter speed can be adjusted for fast-action photography. However, the equivalent to overcranking would be the utilization of a variable-speed playback machine or digital disk recorder to alter the playback speed of a scene. Extremely high-speed overcranking is most often done on film.

overexposure

The result of a purposeful or accidental allowance of excess light onto each film frame, the picture has a somewhat pale, washed-out look.

There are two comparative video equivalents to overexposure. The first would be to turn off a video camera's auto exposure and purposely overexpose the scene. As in film, there is a possibility of image damage if the iris is opened too far, exceeding the videotape's capability to handle excessive light. Another means of overexposing a video image would be the increasing of the luminance levels of the video signal either during or at some point after recording. Luminance levels may be monitored and adjusted using any of several instruments, such as a waveform monitor.

overrun Generally a financial term, referring to going over budget. See also *overage.*

overscan

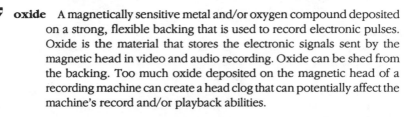

To scan dimensions larger than those visible on a home television screen. There is more picture broadcast in a video signal than is visible on a normal home television. Most home television monitors overscan the video image to ensure that no black, nonsignal border appears. However, visually undesirable portions of the video signal, such as horizontal and vertical blanking, although scanned, are masked simply by the dimensions of the picture tube. Most professional monitors and some home television sets can adjust the viewing range of the picture area. Overscanning the picture thus approximates the viewing area of the average home viewer's television. Underscanning shows the complete picture included in the video signal, including the horizontal and vertical areas that are not considered "positively viewable" on a home television set.

Most wide-screen film formats are blowups of a 35-millimeter image with the top and bottom masked off. The projecting of a properly matted wide-screen format would be similar to overscan.

oxide   A magnetically sensitive metal and/or oxygen compound deposited on a strong, flexible backing that is used to record electronic pulses. Oxide is the material that stores the electronic signals sent by the magnetic head in video and audio recording. Oxide can be shed from the backing. Too much oxide deposited on the magnetic head of a recording machine can create a head clog that can potentially affect the machine's record and/or playback abilities.

Paint Box™

☐ A brand name of the Quantel Corporation's electronic paint system, a type of flexible graphics device. Very sophisticated computerized drawing tools, paint systems allow artists to create images in video, using many of the same types of brush strokes that an artist working on paper would have.

Many paint systems have the capability to animate. With this capability, rotoscoping, that is, hand painting of individual video frames and complicated designs, can be created. Most paint systems also have the ability to capture black-and-white as well as color images from video sources, thus shortening input time and allowing for more creative time on the machine.

➡ Some video systems are capable of rendering onto film. However, the best comparison to a paint system would be single-frame animation and optical printing. Some paint systems have the ability to input live video; thus, this comparison would include production footage optically composited.

☐ **PAL** A technical method of recording and playing back video; used in the United Kingdom and other countries. It displays 25 frames per second (as opposed to 30 frames per second in the U.S.-used system) and has 625 lines of video information per frame (as opposed to 525 lines in the United States). See also *NTSC*.

pan To horizontally pivot the camera sideways without changing its actual position vertically or horizontally.

pan and scan The process of selecting the area of the film frame to show when conforming a wide-screen film format to the smaller 4 to 3 television ratio (Figure 33). Since not all of the wide-screen image can be accommodated by the narrower television field without including black borders at the top and bottom (called a letterbox format), during the telecine process the transferred area of the film must continuously

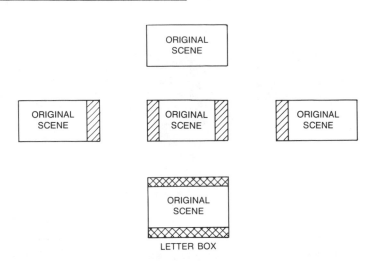

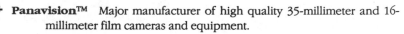

LETTER BOX

Figure 33   Pan and scan. Wide-screen film formats are cropped for televsion viewing. Some portion of the picture is lost in this process. When titles are in the picture, often the letterbox format is used to see the whole frame. However, masks are visible during this time at the top and bottom.

be selected. Scenes encompassing the entire width of the film often are panned. See also *telecine*.

Panavision™   Major manufacturer of high quality 35-millimeter and 16-millimeter film cameras and equipment.

pancake   A flat, rectangular, wooden box used to elevate equipment.

parallax   The difference between what the operator sees through the eyepiece or viewfinder and the image actually being recorded on film; occurs in some, particularly older, cameras not utilizing a reflex viewfinder system. In reflex systems, used almost exclusively in newer cameras and in video cameras, a small portion of the light exposing the film is diverted to the viewfinder; the operator actually sees the image that is being recorded. In parallax systems, the viewfinder does not receive actual image light; its mechanism is distinct from that of the exposure mechanism and approximates the image being recorded. Adjustments are often made to the system to compensate for this difference.

parallel action   Editing two or more stories in a production in such a way that they appear to be occurring at the same time.

patch   To connect equipment electronically through the use of wires and cables.

patch panel   A centralized area specifically configured by the user to connect electronically various pieces of equipment (Figure 34).

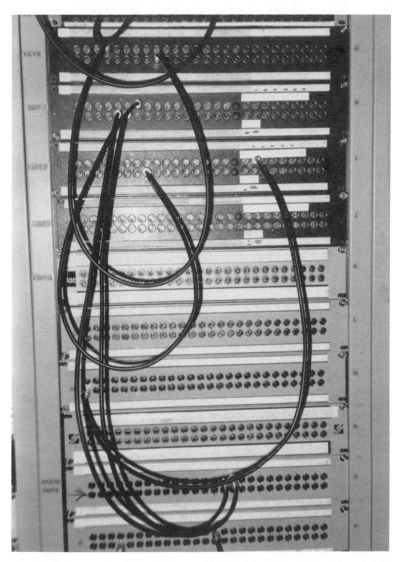

Figure 34   Patch panel. This video patch panel is used to route video signals throughout a facility. Photo to Sean Sterling, courtesy of Video Research Corporation.

pedestal

□ Also called **setup**. The lowest black level technically allowed by the Federal Communications Commission's (FCC) broadcast rules, $7^1/_2$ percent of white level. See also *black level*.

➡ The comparison would be to the fog level or toe in a film's characteristic curve. This is the physical limit of the film stock's darkness sensitivity, whereas the pedestal is the technically defined limits of the video signal in the U.S. broadcast system.

🎥 A sturdy, cylindrical device to which the camera is attached, allowing limited vertical movement of the camera.

🎥 **pegbar** A metal strip with three pins; used for registering animation. Holes are punched in the artwork to accommodate the strip. In some cases, the strip is manipulated by a precision device to create movement of the artwork.

🎥 **per diem** A day-by-day allowance for food and/or room usually paid to workers who are on location.

🎥 **persistence of vision** The physical reaction of the eye that causes the retention of an image after it has actually disappeared. This is how the brain perceives action on the screen (film or video). The eye retains one image, and then, before that image fades, another appears, creating the illusion of one continuous image.

🎥 **phasing** Intentional or unintentional cancellation of portions of an audio signal; the result of combining two sound sources whose frequencies are the same but whose waveforms are slightly displaced in time. The term *phase* specifically refers to the relationship of signals with the same frequency. The waveforms of in-phase signals match perfectly in time. The waveforms of out-of-phase signals do not match to varying degrees, with accompanying amounts of cancellation. Signals in anti-phase completely cancel each other.

Audio is recorded in a certain phase relationship. With more than one track of audio, the tracks can be recorded out of phase with each other, cancelling partially and creating intentionally or unintentionally unusual sounds. If an error, phasing can be corrected by reversing the phase of one of the tracks.

phosphor

▢ The substance that emits light when struck by a form of radiant energy; for instance, a stream of electrons, as in a cathode ray.

➡ The film comparison would be the reflective material of the screen. The television tube or CRT emits light forward toward the audience. The film screen reflects light toward the audience.

🎥 **pickup crew** Local personnel used on a remote location, often meaning a crew that is not necessarily highly skilled.

pickup device

▢ The electronic element that converts an image into an electrical signal. There are various electronic apparatuses that accomplish this task: plumbicon tubes, vidicon tubes, or charged coupled devices (CCDs).

➡ The film pickup device is the emulsion on the film. The emulsion picks up the image, while the processing fixes or stores that image, like the videotape does in the video system.

picture safety area   Also called **safe picture area**. The area of a video signal that approximates the average home viewer's television. There is more picture in a video signal than is visible on a normal home television. The area where titles are considered safely viewable is called safe title.

Pilotone

An electronic pulse-based system used to synchronize production picture and audio. A generator attached to the film camera creates a pulse each time a frame of film is exposed within the camera. The pulse is sent via a cable to the sound recorder and recorded on one of the audio tracks. This pulse, thus, is a record of the speed at which the camera is operating at any specific time. In order to play back the audio recording in sync with the camera speed, a resolver is used to play back the audio. By reading the Pilotone, the resolver continually adjusts the playback speed to match that of the camera when the film was exposed.

➡ Pilotone is a type of control track of the camera recorded on audiotape.

pin registered

A method of providing image stability during photography or projection that inserts a pin into a film sprocket hole as each frame is exposed or projected. This mechanism supplements the pulldown claw that actually advances the film frame by frame.

➡ The pinch roller within the tape transport of a VTR would be comparable to pin registration, as the former stabilizes the moving tape. Pin registration is used to eliminate film weave in transferring to video.

pinch roller

A rubber cylinder that holds video- or audiotape against the capstan in order to transport the tape across the heads at a constant speed. See also *capstan.*

➡ Mechanisms that engage film sprockets and stabilize the film, such as the pulldown claw or pin registration, would be comparable to the pinch roller.

pixillation   An effect created by a series of stills giving the appearance of motion. The effect can be created from actual stills or by freezing frames of moving images for a short (a few frames) period of time.

pizza box   Also called **spot box**. A flat cardboard box and plastic reel used to store and transport small amounts of edited videotape.

playback head   A video or audio head designed for playback (not record) only.

positive image An image with the same colors and densities as the original scene. The opposite would be a negative image.

post dubbing This is the process of adding synchronous sound, especially dialogue, after production has taken place. There are two basic ways that dialogue is added into a film. The first is looping; the second is called automatic dialogue replacement (ADR). The end result of these dubbing sessions is the same: the replacement of the audio recorded during production with audio from a sound facility. The reasons for this replacement could be that an actor's reading is not exactly what the director is looking for; ambient sound has ruined the take; the original take is not available, for whatever reason; and so on. See also *automatic dialogue replacement; looping.*

post-production All audio, video, film, and other activities that occur between the end of production and delivery of the program. This includes, but is not limited to, editing, creating audio and visual effects, mixing, scoring, titling, looping, screenings, remixing, dubbing, and negative cutting.

post-score To compose music, with or without lyrics, after the production is completed. Even on a feature film, the composer may work with a videotape, as the home video player has become common.

POV Abbreviation for *point of view.* The abbreviation is used as much as, if not more than, the actual words. The term is often used to describe a shot that is designed to be the image that a character would be viewing. For example, if a character were looking at a building, the POV of that character would be a shot of the building taken from where the character was standing.

preamplifier A device designed to increase weak signals. A preamplifier is often used when a microphone is being patched directly into an amplifier.

prelay
□ The audio process of preparing audio for a mix. This includes locating audio, premixing audio sources, cleaning dialogue, and laying sources down onto a multitrack.
⇌ These prelay chores are the functions of the dialogue, effects, and music editors who prepare such specific tracks for the dubbing sessions.

premix An audio mix that takes place before a final mix. For example, a premix might combine several sound-effects tracks down to a single track prior to final mixing.

pre-production All chores pertaining to the production that occur before the shooting of footage. This might include, but is not limited to, storyboarding, writing, production planning, budgeting, casting, location scouting, prerecording, equipment rental, scheduling, rewriting, and incorporation.

prerecord   To record music or other sources of audio before production of a scene begins. This audio is used for playback on the set during production. For example, musical numbers and music videos usually are shot while playing back a piece of music to which actors or musicians respond.

preroll

☐ The distance a video- or audiotape machine must be backed up in order to achieve normal speed and/or synchronize by the time a recording or playback is to take place.

⇒ The film comparison would be lock-up or lock-up time.

pressure plate   A basically flat piece of metal that holds the moving film firmly against the gate as it is exposed within the camera. The pressure plate is designed so that it touches only the edges of the film, minimizing the chance that the area of film being exposed will be scratched.

preview

🎥 A screening before a film is officially released; used as a test of an audience's reaction to the film. This process allows for last-minute changes in the film or in the marketing strategy of that film.

☐ A practice edit that shows what the edit would look like without recording the edit. Random-access editing systems work on the principal of previewing a series of edits.

primary colors   See *colors, primary.*

prime lens   A fixed-focal-length lens, as opposed to a zoom lens, which has a variable focal length.

prime time   Those hours during the day when the family is usually at home and most likely to watch television. *Prime time* is defined as between 8 PM and 11 PM in the Eastern and Pacific time zones and between 7 PM and 10 PM in the Central and Mountain time zones.

print

1. A copy of another piece of film, generally a positive copy, usually made for projection in a theater.
2. To make a positive copy for editing purposes. Not all takes that are shot are copied onto positive film for post-production use. At the end of an acceptable take, a director might say "That's a print" or "Print it," indicating to the camera crew to make a positive copy for the editor. These takes that are meant to be printed are called circled takes.

printer

The device that creates the release prints, the work print, and the opticals for film. Although there are several types of film printers, their purposes are the same: to duplicate the image from one piece of film to another.

The *continuous contact printer* is used for release prints and work prints. Because the film is fed through the printer without stopping, the continuous printer is ideal for situations where image quality is not acutely critical. Because the continuous printer is relatively fast, it is used for the hundreds, if not thousands, of release prints needed in the theaters.

The *step contact printer* derives its name from the fact that it comes to a complete halt at each frame. This printer produces sharper pictures than the continuous printer but is much slower (and, therefore, more expensive). Because of this slowness, the step contact printer is used when image quality is the dominant factor in the print, such as in creating internegatives and interpositives.

The *optical printer* is used to create a varied group of effects. Optical printers are basically a camera and a projector housed in one unit, perfectly aligned, with the ability to move both the source footage and raw stock film in sync. Lenses are used in the optical printer to achieve some of its effects. Fade-ins and fade-outs are performed on optical printers.

There are two types of optical printers: continuous contact and step optical. The step optical printer is responsible for creating the more complicated optical effects (Figure 35). The step optical printer is capable of anything that the production camera can do and more because it has all the controls that the production camera has plus the ability to expose raw stock to an image with frame-accurate control.

The world of video effects has a number of effects devices that create effects, rather than just a variation on one (Table 8).

In the video world, a printer is the same as the printer in the computer world; it is a device that prints out information (usually the edit decision list) on paper.

printing dupe

An internegative, usually a timed internegative derived from a timed interpositive. The printing dupe is used to create the projection prints.

The equivalent is the edited master, the source of all the delivery and/ or broadcast masters.

print-through Unintentional transfer of information from one layer of material to another adjacent layer on a reel. This can occur with video- or audiotape.

proc amp See *processing amplifier.*

GATE   GATES   EYE PIECE FOR VIEWING

Figure 35 A step optical printer. Note the two supply and take-up reels above the two gates. The two optical elements allow for the alignment of two film elements (like a hold-out matte and background) at one time. Photo by Sean Sterling, courtesy of Cinema Research Corporation.

Table 8. Video Effects Devices

Generic Name	Effects Use
switcher	dissolves, wipes, title keying, chroma keys/blue screen
digital video effects	image reposition, reductions and blowups, freeze frames
digital disk recorder	layering, more than three times variable speed forward or more than one times reverse
variable-speed playback deck	freeze frames, variable-speed playback three times forward, one times reverse
paint/graphics system	complicated rotoscoping, animation, frame touch-up, specialized drawings

processing amplifier (proc amp)

☐ An electronic device designed to remove synchronization pulses in a video signal and replace them with newly formed signals. The primary use of this ability is to fill in missing synchronization signals and replace faulty ones. Cameras often have these protective and often adjustable circuits built in. A proc amp also acts as a gate, preventing extremely bright video levels (levels that might overload a video circuit) from being recorded. Finally, a processing amplifier may offer other controls, allowing a user to modify a signal's technical characteristics, such as chrominance and luminance levels. See also *clipping*.

⇌ There is neither a piece of film equipment nor a film process that is analogous, as the film stock acts as its own proc amp. When too much light is introduced to film, the image simply becomes overexposed. As a result, the silver halides surrounding the image are damaged by the spillover of light. This result is occasionally used as an effect.

projection　To convert an image in electronic or chemical form into illuminated (light) form that can be directed to and focused upon a display medium, such as a screen. Film is projected by shining white light through the dye-laden base. Video is projected, respectively, within or outside of a cathode ray tube by three electron guns or projecting lens units, one each of red, green, and blue.

projector

A machine that moves a long piece of film along a path and first shines a powerful light through the film and then, immediately after, decodes the audio track (Figure 36). This slight delay compensates for the additional time needed for the picture to be projected onto a distant screen. The film projector is similar to the camera in its physical handling of film. The sound may be recorded on a magnetic track or an optical track.

There is a special type of projector that is used to view work prints and that is called an interlock projector. Since a work print has the audio track separate from the picture, the projector needs two drive systems. Both sides of the interlock are mechanically geared together, so that when the picture is viewed, the sound is run in sync.

⇌ The projector and auditorium in film are comparable to the CRT or television and the room in which it is viewed (Figure 36). The image is projected as in film, only the audience is outside the viewing system.

Another more obvious comparison to the film projector is the video projector. Sometimes referred to as projection television, this technique commonly employs three coordinated lens projectors, one each for the primary light colors, red, green, and blue. However, its resolution is generally inferior to the quality of the film projector or regular television.

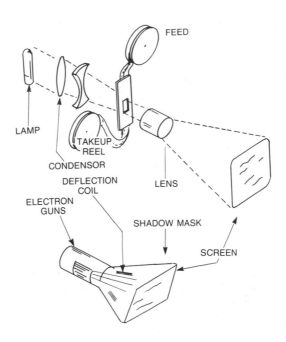

Figure 36 Projector and CRT. The projector and television tube are similar in concept. The audience is on the outside of the screening system in video and inside the screen system (an auditorium) when viewing film.

protection master
- Also called **safety master** or **submaster**. A dub (duplicate) of any videotape used for archival or protection purposes. Usually a protection master is created from a final edited master, a special effects master, or any tape that is deemed irreplaceable.
- There are two protections involved in film production, generally called protection prints. The protection interpositive (IP) is printed from the cut negative in order to protect the film in the event the cut negative is lost or damaged. In addition, once the internegative is created from the timed interpositive, the timed interpositive is stored for protection in case the internegative is damaged in any way.

proxar A supplemental lens that shortens the focal length of the lens being used.

pull reel
- Also called **select reel**. A reel of scenes or takes selected, by the

director, producer, or other production staff, and recorded onto another reel for viewing or editing purposes.

⇐ The equivalent would be the circled takes selected by the director during production, which then are printed as dailies. In video production, every take is printed.

pulldown claw

The mechanism that advances the film through the camera one frame at a time by engaging the film's perforations at regular intervals. Because the film perforations are at equal intervals, the claw regularly engages the film and advances it the same distance with each stroke or cycle.

⇐ The videotape machine uses a capstan, which is a precision metal roller, to pinch the tape against a plastic roller and move the tape across video heads at a stable speed.

pushing film

A laboratory process in which film underexposed during the production process is corrected by either leaving it for a longer time in the developer or by increasing the temperature of the developer. This results in increasing the film's contrast ratio during the developing stage. See also *forced development.*

⇐ The comparison would be to alter the black and/or white levels of the video playback during the editing process, thus altering the contrast level of the original footage.

☐ **Quad** See *quadruplex*.

☐ **quadruplex (quad)** An early (1956) method of recording videotape, now nearly obsolete. This system employed four (quad) video record heads and two-inch-wide tape. It is not commonly used in broadcast situations.

R – Y (R minus Y)   The color difference signal that is the result of the subtraction of the luminance signal (Y) from the red signal (R).

rack

1. A large metal shelf that is used to store film vertically.
2. To thread film in an editing system or camera. An editor might say, "Rack up reel three on the Steinbeck."

A metal frame onto which electronic gear is attached, for example, several VTRs and monitors. There are consumer racks being marketed in audio/video speciality stores.

rack-over   Technique in primarily older, nonreflex film cameras in which a viewfinder separated from the lens system is pivoted to join the system, allowing operators to accurately confirm framing and other characteristics of the shot. See also *reflex camera*.

radio frequency (rf)   A type of electromagnetic radiation used to encode and transmit broadcast signals through modulation. Video recordings are modulated to radio waves as part of the television transmission process.

random-access editing

A feature of certain advanced video post-production systems that enables a user to independently modify (lengthen, shorten, move, etc.) any segment of an editing project without having to make accommodating adjustments to the rest of the program. A random-access editing system generally consists of a centralized computer that coordinates a number of video storage devices. Until the edited version is actively finalized and copied onto a release medium, an editor's decisions are simply held as a list of instructions within the computer's memory. Thus, the editor can easily modify the list, and the computer automatically will adapt the other elements on the list to each change. For example, if an editor shortens a shot, the computer automatically moves up the next shot, eliminating a potential gap. Random-access editing systems typically offer a preview mode, enabling editors to see the segments produced by different editing decisions.

There are two basic types of random-access editing systems: disk-based and tape-based systems. Tape-based random-access editing systems coordinate a group of source video cassette decks (Figure 37). Often, several decks contain identical source material; because of the slow access time of videotape players, the system usually needs such multiple copies to quickly play back video located on different parts of the tape. As it previews edits, the system identifies for each segment which of several identical source videos is positioned closest to the segment to be played back and engages that source.

The disk-based system has fewer playback sources than the video system, since the laser disks have a much faster access time. During preview, the system's computer determines which playback deck is closest to the next edit and positions the source before the currently previewed edit is completed.

 Picture editing in film is a nonlinear process. However, once complicated sound tracks are built for the final mix, difficulties arise in any

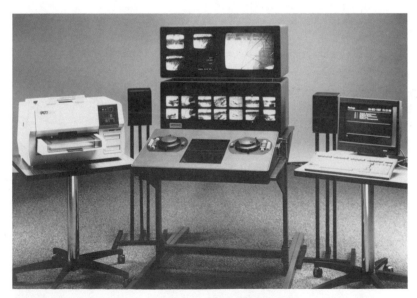

Figure 37   Montage Picture Processor. The Montage Picture Processor (Series II) is a random-access electronic editing system. It is a tape-based processor using several videotapes, as well as digital processing, to achieve random-access editing of footage. To the extreme left is an optical laser printer for story boards. Photo courtesy of Charles J. Lepow, Inc.

picture change that is made. If a picture change is made, all the tracks for that reel must be altered by the same amount, an involved and time-consuming process. For this reason, some feature films are transferred to video for post-production so they more easily can be edited nonlinearly.

range finder　An instrument that calculates the distance from the device to a specific object. This type of instrument is also found in most 35-millimeter still cameras to determine focus.

Rank Cintel　A top-of-the-line telecine manufactured by Rank. Rank's telecines operate on the principal of using a light source emanating from a cathode ray tube (CRT) giving the device the name *flying spot scanner.* See also *electron beam recording; flying spot scanner; telecine.*

raster
- The horizontal line pattern on the face of a CRT or video tube. See also *interlace; scanning.*
- The film analogy is the front of the theater screen onto which the light from the projector is thrown.

raw stock
- Unexposed film, one that has no image on it and has not been exposed to any light.
- Blank videotape that has not had any recording on it. Blank tape has no control track, picture, or other information on it. When played back in a tape machine, one sees either nothing or a speckled display called snow.

rear-screen projection　The projection of a still or moving picture onto a screen behind the action that is being photographed. This technique can seemingly put characters into the locale or action of the projected scene while still shooting in the studio.

recans
- Film that has been in a camera, but not exposed. See also *short end.*
- Videotape can be reused. However, repeated use increases the chance of tape damage or dropouts. Camera original footage should be, if at all possible, new stock. Window dubs and B reel stock could be made using used stock if the stock has not seen too much previous use.

receiver　A device that is designed to pick up and convert broadcast signals. Examples of these devices would be radios, televisions, wireless microphones, and walkie-talkies. See also *radio frequency.*

receiver/monitor　A television set designed to pick up and display both over-the-air (broadcast) signals and video signals. The term also indicates a higher quality device than a normal television set. A set wired for cable is not necessarily video ready because a cable signal is a modulated signal. See also *modulation; radio frequency.*

▢ **record button**

1. The button on a video record machine that initiates the record process. Usually the play button and the record button must be pressed simultaneously in order to begin the recording (which begins an assemble recording).

2. The little red button on the bottom of three-quarter-inch tape cassettes. When the button is in place, a recording can be made. If the button is removed, a record machine will not record on that tape. VHS and audiotapes have a similar device called a record tab.

recordist

🎥 The person in charge of recording production audio.

⇒ The video term would be the *sound person.*

🎥 **red pencil**   To mark for deletion.

reel summary

▢ A computer printout or handwritten list indicating what playback sources will be needed to on-line a program.

⇒ The film negative cut list is a reel summary, indicating what footage will need to be pulled for conforming.

📹 **reflectance exposure meter**   A device that measures the intensity of light reflected from an object. See also *incidence exposure meter.*

reflex camera

🎥 A film camera designed so the operator sees the exact same image that is striking the film. Reflex still cameras use mirrors that move at the moment of picture taking to allow the operator to see the image to be photographed. Movie cameras usually have a mirror that reflects some of the light passing through the lens to the eyepiece.

⇒ Essentially the video camera is a reflex camera, as the picture on the monitor is the same image that lands on the pickup tube or CCD and is subsequently sent on to the record machine.

📹 **regenerated time code**   A duplicated time code that is created, rather than just copied. If time code is merely copied to another tape, the copied signal can be too noisy or too distorted to be decoded. To avoid this problem, time code should be fed into a device that reads the old time code, then creates (regenerates) a new, clean digital signal for recording.

registration pin

🎥 A device built into a motion picture camera that engages the film's sprocket holes after the film has been positioned by the pulldown claw. The purpose of the registration pin is to hold the film firmly in place during exposure.

⇒ Videotape does not stop in its travels across the record head. It is positioned while moving by the tension from the pull of the capstan and pinch roller and the pressure of the tension arm on the feed side of the supply reel.

release print
- A print of a program that is for distribution. Prints are most often made from an internegative or a color reversal intermediate (CRI).
- The video equivalent of a release print would be an air copy.

rerecordist
- The person in charge of mixing the tracks of audio.
- The video term for this person would be a *mixer*.

resolution The ability to recreate detail in an electronic or film recording medium. The higher the number of lines of resolution, the more precise the reproduction of the actual scene. Charts are photographed to determine the resolution of any particular camera, screen, or monitor.

resolver A device that decodes a Pilotone or other audio signal and allows an audio playback device to replay a tape at the same speed as it was recorded. This is needed for transferring film-production audio when a synchronous motor is used. It is also used in production audio playback scenes where the lip sync of performers must stay constant with each take.

reversal stock Film stock that, after processing, yields an image of the same type as that to which it was originally exposed. For example, a reversal stock used to film a scene would produce a positive image, and a reversal stock printed from a negative would produce a duplicate negative. Video, given its electronic nature, would generally not involve a distinction between positive and negative images.

reverse angle A shot in which the camera is placed within the frame of a previous shot and aimed in the direction where the camera used to be.

rewind
- To move film, videotape, or audiotape backward by the use of some mechanical or electronic device.
- A device bolted to a bench that has handles on it and is used, generally during post-production, to wind film through gang synchronizers.
- The video comparison would be a playback or record deck, the device that transports videotape and is used in the editing process.

rf See *radio frequency*.

rgb Abbreviation of the three primary colors of light: red, green, and blue; often expressed in that order.

ribbon microphone A microphone whose pickup element is a ribbon or corrugated metal foil stretched between positively and negatively charged magnets. Sound waves cause the foil to vibrate, creating an electromagnetic current analogous to the original sound.

ringing

☐ The apparent aberration surrounding small letters or designs in a video signal. This is caused by the television signal's inability to quickly adjust from one frequency to another and back again without some distortion. This irregularity is often seen at the end of movie commercials where there are numerous small letters.

⇐ Ringing in film is caused by a flawed or misadjusted optical system and, thus, does not have the same source as video ringing. However, the visual result of this film defect approximates the look of ringing.

roll cameras/roll tape Director's cue to start recording.

room tone The sound that occurs naturally in any given room without people talking. See also *ambient sound*.

roster A list of production and other staff with their duties, abilities, or union classifications.

Rotoscope™

🎥 Trade name for a device that projects film image onto a table specifically designed for animation. This set-up allows an animator to draw animation cels in relation to the actual production footage, one frame at a time.

☐ This term has come to indicate any single-frame treatment of a visual project; so using a paint or graphics system to animate, or treat, frames is referred to as rotoscoping.

rough Incomplete, not in a final form; for example, rough audio, rough cut, rough mix. Basically a draft or temporary attempt at some effect, aurally or visually.

rough cut

🎥 A preliminary assembly of all the film's elements in their script order. Timing and pacing are not yet perfected, and scenes are often added, deleted, and changed after the rough cut.

☐ Each version of a work print of a show is called a rough cut. The way each successive version is delineated would be by number (cut one, cut two) and by date.

Since video footage is not physically separated from the reel of tape, a rough cut in the film sense is not usually performed.

Occasionally there is a need to pull selected takes from various sources and edit them onto another reel. This process would be *making a pull reel* or *making a select reel*. The pull reel, if properly made, could be used in the final assembly; however, time code and reel designation would probably be different from the camera original reel(s).

☐ **router** A device that accepts signal input from a variety of pieces of equipment and that can be directed to send that information to another piece of equipment by remote control; an automated patch bay.

rubber numbers

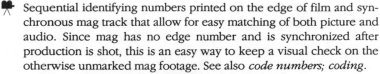

Sequential identifying numbers printed on the edge of film and synchronous mag track that allow for easy matching of both picture and audio. Since mag has no edge number and is synchronized after production is shot, this is an easy way to keep a visual check on the otherwise unmarked mag footage. See also *code numbers; coding*.

The actual window in the window dub would compare to rubber numbers. The production time code is visibly etched in the work-print footage, allowing easy access to the time code of the synchronous audio track or surrounding footage. Audio, however, unlike rubber numbers, has no *visible* time code reference.

run out

Protective leader at the end of a film reel whose sole purpose is to protect the body of the reel.

In video, run out would be called the tail of the reel.

run through   A practice or a rehearsal, sometimes with equipment at the ready, sometimes without any of the technical crew available.

running shot   A shot taken by a camera mounted on some movable platform that moves rapidly to keep up with an action scene. See also *dolly; tracking shot*.

running time

The length of a show, tape, or take. The running time in video is often referred to in actual time.

The length of edited film is usually referred to in terms of feet or feet and frames.

rushes   A day's or production's unedited footage. In film, this footage is also called dailies.

safe picture area   See *picture safety area.*

safe title area   That part of a television screen where titles are considered safely viewable at home. Some of the viewing area is *unsafe* because there is more picture in a video signal than is visible on a normal home television. See also *picture safety area.*

safety master   See *protection master.*

save the lights/save the camera   A cue to turn off the lights or camera.

scale   The lowest pay scale of any union classification. Although a production company may pay any worker more than scale, scale is the least the company can pay for that particular position.

scan
1. To run through footage at a high speed.
2. The way a cathode ray moves across the face of a cathode ray tube. See also *blanking; cathode ray tube; raster; scanning.*

scanning

The process by which a video signal is converted into an image that is displayed on the inner surface of a cathode ray tube. A stream of electrons emitted by an electron gun within a tube precisely traces this inner surface in a pattern of horizontal lines, illuminating phosphors coating the inner surface and creating the image.

In the NTSC standard video system, a total of 525 scan lines of information composes one frame of video. However, the frame actually consists of two fields, each comprised of 262.5 lines, that are combined (interlaced) to create the full frame.

The scanning process also is utilized, although essentially in reverse, in the conversion of images to video signals within a video camera.

Note that, although the electron beam is intermittent (it scans one line and one field at a time), the scanning process is basically more continuous than the intermittent pulldown process in film. See also *blanking; cathode ray.*

⇌ The film equivalent to scanning is projection. Whereas the video image is displayed on the face of a tube, the film image is projected onto a large screen. The scanning process itself is equal to the image's reflection off the screen.

scene

1. A segment of a program that takes place in one apparently continuous uninterrupted action. A program is built by combining a series of scenes.

2. A segment of a show that occurs in one area, time, or place.

scenery dock   That area where set pieces are stored.

score   The musical portion of a production.

scratch

🎥 Damage caused by physical marring of the emulsion of the film, resulting in a visible elimination of picture. When projected, a scratch is often 10,000 times larger than its original size. The emulsion on the face of the acetate backing is extremely fragile.

⇌ A video dropout would be the equivalent of a film scratch. A dropout is a lack of oxide on the videotape. In that area on the tape, there is no picture information. Dropout compensators, usually found in video time base correctors, attempt to correct these errors.

▢ Videotape can become scratched due to improper handling or a damaged head. Scratches cause extremely large dropouts.

scratch track   A temporary audio track often used for editing.

screen

🎥 Highly reflective material onto which light is projected. That light is reflected back toward an audience.

▢ The common video *screen* is not a reflective material but a phosphorous material on the inner surface of a cathode ray tube that glows when struck by electrons; it is used to project (forward) a moving or still image.

screening

🎥 The viewing of a film project, usually involving a projection room. However, the viewing of a film on a flatbed occasionally is referred to as a screening.

▢ The viewing of a video project, usually in a viewing room or edit bay.

script   The written plan of a program. Industrial (nonbroadcast, nontheatrical) scripts are often written with dialogue on one side of the page and the visuals on the other. Feature-film and television scripts are mostly scene setups and dialogue and have little picture information. A shooting script, the director's plan for shooting the program, is the detailed plan of how the production is to be shot.

script breakdown
1. To financially estimate the cost of a production by analyzing the program's script and its requirements.
2. A shooting script and call sheet created by examining and dissecting a program's script.

SECAM   A technical method of recording video used in Europe; vastly different from the United States' system of video recording, called NTSC. See also *formats; NTSC; PAL*.

secondary colors   See *colors, secondary*.

select reel   See *pull reel*.

setup   To technically prepare for a scene.

setup   See *pedestal*.

shadow mask   See *aperture mask*.

shedding

☐ Separation of oxide from the videotape base. The result of shedding is a dramatic increase of dropouts. Videotape that has begun to shed should be discarded as soon as possible. See also *dropout*.

⇐ A direct comparison would be the emulsion separating from the film base. A more practical comparison would be a green print, a processed film that has excess humidity in the emulsion, which can create damage or unsteadiness when run through a projector.

short end

That portion of unexposed film left over from a full reel. Short ends can be bought for production use for less money than full reels, but care must be taken because short-end footage could have been flashed or inadvertently exposed.

⇐ The video equivalent is cutdown stock, the remainder of a longer reel that was not used by a facility's previous client. A video short end might be used for a commercial since, for such a production, including bars, tone, slate, commercial, head, and tail leader, only five minutes of tape is needed; yet most videotape comes in half-hour or hour reels.

shotgun microphone   A highly directional microphone that is physically very long and narrow. The shotgun mike is aimed at the performer, giving the impression of a shotgun.

single-stripe film   A film that has one oxide stripe available for an audio track. Looking at single-stripe film, there is a second stripe of oxide to balance the thickness of the first stripe. See also *balance stripe; magnetic film; three-stripe film.*

skew   A distortion at the top of a television picture due to improper tension as the tape moves across the heads. If the problem has occurred during the recording process, the distortion may be uncorrectable. One possible solution would be to play back that tape on the same machine that it was recorded on. If the error is occurring during playback, adjusting the tracking on the playback deck may correct the problem.

slant track   An older term referring to *helical scan recording.* This is a recording in which the heads cross the videotape at an angle allowing for a longer area of recording and is used in all video formats except two-inch tape.

slate
Provided during production, an aural and/or visual identification of the shot or take that follows.

Most often-used slate is a **clapstick,** or clapperboard, a device onto which one can write permanent shot information. See also *clapsticks.*

The ease of using the clapboard for visual identification (as opposed to using a piece of paper) has fostered its adoption by video personnel. Slates for edited tape programs or segments are recorded on the front of the program using a character generator (a type of electronic typewriter).

slave
1. To lock or reference one machine to another, usually through use of a computer and the videotape's time code. Multiple record masters can be made with no generational loss by slaving one record machine to another.
2. To lock a time code generator to another time code source. See also *slaved time code.*

slaved time code
Time code that is taken from a source videotape and fed into a time code regenerator, which replicates the source code. This process is used to continue ceased time code, replace erased or faulty time code, or to create a dub or window dub of the original tape.

The film equivalent would be either striking a work print with key numbers of the original negative or recoding a replaced work print with the same code as the original.

slow motion
Reducing the speed of action either in production, by exposing more frames per second than normal sound speed, or in post-production, through the use of an optical printer. By repeating an image during exposure, motion is slowed down. The optical printer is capable of

various printing patterns to achieve different speeds of slow motion. See also *overcranking; printer (optical)*.

▢ Through the use of a dynamic tracking videotape playback machine, video can achieve a slow motion effect. A tape machine is only capable of three times sound speed forward and one times sound speed in reverse. Any faster than this would require using a digital disk recorder.

slug

▢ The space left for a commercial break or other element in a tape program. It is not unusual for the slug to be less than the actual time for the program material being inserted.

⇌ A banner is placed in a program where material is missing. In the picture, leader is placed in the area of missing images, perhaps from a lost trim. On the audio track(s), old or unnecessary picture is used for the slug. See also *banner*.

sof

🎥 Abbreviation for *sound on film*, referring to synchronized picture and sound together on one film.

⇌ Video is *sound on tape* (sot).

sot

▢ Abbreviation for *sound on tape*, often referring to sync sound on tape.

⇌ Film would be *sound on film* (sof).

🎥 **sound report**   The written log that comes from the sound recordist; made during the production. This account gives details of problems and notations from the set.

🎬 **sound speed**   A reference to running film or tape at standard speed for any format. Film is either 24 or 30 frames per second. NTSC video is approximately 30 frames per second. See also *frame rate*.

🎥 **sound stage**   A high-ceilinged, large building specifically built to shoot sound films. The interior of the building is designed for film production, from the grid in the ceiling to facilitate lighting to the huge doors allowing set pieces to be easily moved in and out. See also *studio*.

🎬 **sound track**   The musical portion of a film or taped program released on an audio cassette, LP, or compact disk.

🎥 **soup**   The developing solutions used to process unexposed film.

🎥 **splice**   The joining together of two separate pieces of film. See also *cement splice; splicer; tape splice*.

splicer

🎥 A device that locks two pieces of film in place to allow for a tape or cement attachment to occur. There are two types of splicers: cement and tape.

Figure 38   A well worn cement splicer. Note the film wound around the plastic core to the left of the splicer. Photo by Sean Sterling, courtesy of Cinema Research Corporation.

The *cement splicer* forms a physical and chemical join of two pieces of film (Figure 38). A specially designed blade on the splicer is used to scrape some emulsion off the end of one piece of film so the two pieces can be cemented together. A heating element in the splicer speeds the curing of the cement. Because of the small, unnoticeable overlap, the cement splicing process requires the loss of two film frames per slice. Once a cement splice has been made the only way it can be undone is to lose the two frames involved in the splice.

The *tape splicer*, also called a butt splicer, uses Mylar tape to directly connect the two pieces of film together without any overlap.

 Since video is not physically cut, the equivalent to a splice would be the recorded edit on a standard video editing system.

More specifically, since cement splicing is part of a final editing stage, a video parallel would be with on-line editing, during which camera original footage is conformed to off-line editing decisions. Similarly, tape splicing, part of work-print decision making, is comparable to off-line editing, in which a final edit decision list is generated.

split edit   An audio and picture edit where either the audio or picture leads the synchronous edit. This type of edit is used a great deal by both film and video editors to speed the apparent pace of dialogue-driven scenes. This technique is also used for shock, leading a loud audio sound moments before picture changes. See also *L cut*.

split reels The metal sides used to wind or rewind film that is on a core or to transfer film that needs to be put on a core. The flatbed table has lessened the need to use split reels for a good part of the editing process. See also *core*.

split screen A special effect by which several images are displayed at once on the screen, which is usually divided by a vertical or diagonal line. Phone conversations are a common use for split screens, with each character occupying half the screen. Film and video go about creating split screens in different technical manners. See also *effects; on-line; opticals*.

spot box See *pizza box*.

spotting The choosing of exact audio placement while viewing a program.

spreader A device to stabilize and separate the legs of a camera tripod.

sprocket holes
Physical holes on the sides of the film used by the projector, editing machine, or other film machine to transport the film through the machine. Sprocket holes must be consistent in size and spacing to insure that the motion of the film is constant. Film comes from the manufacturer with the sprocket holes already cut into the film. See also *pulldown claw; registration pin*.

Control track is the video sprocket hole. Control track is an electronic signal placed on the tape by the recording machine in an assemble recording whose purpose is to indicate the optimum speed for playback.

standards conversions
Taking a video signal from one country's format and electronically converting it to another country's format. Usually this type of conversion has the drawback of being slightly fuzzy due to the process involved in the electronics. See also *NTSC; PAL; SECAM*.

A bump from one gauge to another would be similar to a standards conversion. Going to a larger format is not as effective as a transfer to a smaller gauge film.

Steadicam™ A trademarked camera-stabilizing device that attaches to the human body, allowing the camera to float alongside the operator even in situation like moving rapidly across uneven ground or running up stairs.

Steinbeck™ Brand name of a flatbed editing machine. See also *flatbed*.

sticks
1. The term for a camera identifying slate; a shortened word for *clapsticks*. See also *clapsticks; slate*.
2. An inexpensive tripod made out of wood; used to support a camera.

still   A single stationary picture, usually meaning a photograph rather than a motion picture.

stock

The physical recording medium on which an image or sound is stored.

Color film stock is a photographic storage medium composed of a backing (acetate) and generally three layers of light-sensitive silver halides and dyes. (As the film is exposed to light, the silver halides are struck by light photons. During processing the halides struck by these photons are dyed, resulting in a permanent image.)

TYPES OF STOCK

Print stock.

Print stock is low-speed, fine-grained film used to make photographic copies, most often positive images. Low-contrast print stock is used for television because TV has a much lower contrast ratio than that of a film being projected. Also, a theater using a Xenon lamp projector will compensate for the Xenon's bluish color by using print stock with a reddish tint.

Production stock.

Film actually exposed within a camera during a production, usually a negative stock that is of an average gradient of 45 degrees, medium speed, and probably between 75 and 125 ASA, making it fine grained.

Videotape.

Videotape is an electronic storage medium. Similar in construction to audiotape, videotape is composed of a base of Mylar, then a layer of easily magnetized material called oxide. Signals are received by the video recorder, modulated onto a radio frequency, and recorded onto the videotape.

Videotape is usually purchased either blank (having no recorded signal on the tape), or black and coded (the tape has the color black, no audio, and time code recorded onto the entire length of the tape).

 strike

1. To put away. To strike a set is to take it down.
2. A union refusing to work due to a labor disagreement.

studio

That area where a film company is physically located. In most cases, this area also includes the physical buildings where production takes place. However, there are cases where the film studio is more a corporate office than a place where movies are shot.

The video equivalent is called whatever the company is described as: network, station, or studio (if the show is being shot at an independently operated video facility).

The building made specifically for the purpose of shooting programs. This can be an independent studio, television station, or network.

Usually the studio has specific design structures that make it ideal for production: high ceilings, insulated walls, lighting grids, and additional power considerations.

⇒ The film equivalent is called a stage or sound stage.

☐ **submaster**   See *protection master.*

subtitling

🎬 The process of translating the original language of a film or video to another language and then titling the film or video program in the second language. The actual titling process of the two mediums are a little different. Note that sometimes subtitling is avoided by providing for a foreign distributor the picture component and a separate sound track containing all audio elements except the dialogue. The foreign distributor can then add foreign-language dialogue lip synched as closely as possible.

🎥 Visually, the film titling process would be to create an art card, shoot the art card on high-contrast film (hi-con), then run the film (probably a timed negative) and hi-con through an optical printer, creating a new subtitled film.

☐ The video process would be to prepare the subtitles electronically and then, using a dubbing master, convert the program into the broadcast format of another country while subtitling in the language of that country. If it is not possible to title and standards convert at the same time, the chores are separated, with the titling occurring after the program is transferred to the new format.

🎥 **subtractive color system**   The process of using complementary colors (yellow, magenta, and cyan) to create the rest of the spectrum of color. Film utilizes this process in its approach to creating colors. This subtractive process is based on the interaction of substances—in this case, colored dyes—with white light. The color dyes on film absorb specific colors or color ranges from the white light passing through it, allowing only the desired color light to be projected. The complementary colors in film refer to the colors of the dye.

Video, on the other hand, uses an additive color process, combining the primary light colors, red, green, and blue, to create the rest of the color spectrum. These colors refer to the color of the light itself and, when combined, create white light.

superimpose (super)

🎥 An inexpensive method of creating titles or adding graphics. By A/B rolling titles and backgrounds, that is, by combining them within an optical printer, the title will be exposed onto the print. Larger budget films will have their titles prepared at an optical lab.

☐ In the early days of television, titles that appeared in a show were half faded onto the picture. This method was called a *super.* Later, when keys were introduced, the name *super* was still occasionally used for any process of placing titles over picture.

SVHS

□   A technical improvement over VHS home-video format. VHS tapes will play on SVHS equipment. VHS recordings will not play on SVHS equipment. In terms of the hierarchy, SVHS falls between VHS and professional half-inch formats (Betacam and MII).

⇌   Film equivalent would be between super 8 and 16-millimeter film.

sweetening

□   The audio post-production process in which all production audio, dialogue, music, effects, and other sound elements are matched against the video picture and ultimately combined to create the final sound track. Sweetening generally is done on a multitrack audio tape recorder or digital audio workstation (DAW).

In the sweetening bay, the production audio and matching time code from the edited master are laid down, or transferred to the audio multitrack. If there are two tracks of audio on the video edited master, then each of the tracks is laid separately onto the multitrack. In addition, a video dub is made for visual reference while mixing, avoiding wear and tear on the edited master.

Now, music, effects, and narration are placed in their respective channels on the multitrack. As a rule, each type of audio has its own discrete track on the multitrack. Once all the elements are in place, clean of any unneeded heads and tails, at their proper level and equalization, a mix is performed, during which the different audio elements are blended into one final track. When the mix has been approved, the audio is laid back to the edited master.

If there is a time constraint, a final work print could be sent to sweetening instead of the edited master. If a picture change is then made and the show's length is altered, then all the sweetening cues match points between picture and sound would be changed. However, if care is taken, the sweetening process can proceed either during or before the picture is finalized during the on-line.

⇌   Film also undergoes an extensive audio post-production process, although it differs in many ways from that of video. Film sound editors prepare numerous different sound tracks for different sound components, as in video. The final procedure in which these sounds are combined is often called a mix, performed on a dugging stage. However, the video term *sweetening* tends to be broader than any one film procedure.

switcher

□   An electronic device that combines numerous video sources, sometimes through the use of special effects, into one signal (Figure 39). Switchers can be simple, with few capabilities and only a few inputs, or extremely

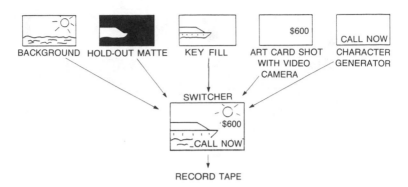

BACKGROUND HOLD-OUT MATTE KEY FILL ART CARD SHOT WITH VIDEO CAMERA CHARACTER GENERATOR

SWITCHER

RECORD TAPE

Figure 39 Switcher combining sources. The purpose of the switcher is to send one composited video picture to the record machine. This process often means combining effects and sources.

large and complex. The switcher is the heart of the on-line editing bay and is also the most important element of a live video broadcast.

⟺ Many of the effects created with the use of the optical printer are found in the switcher: dissolves, wipes, title keying, and chroma key (blue screen).

sync

🎬 Maintaining the corresponding relationship between sound track and picture. See also *lip sync; out of sync.*

📺 The coordination of the vertical and horizontal blanking pulses with the electron beam of a television or camera so that the picture remains stable both horizontally and vertically. See also *blanking; scan.*

⟺ The equivalent would be to physically align the projector or camera, making sure the gate, pulldown claw and pressure plate, and so on, are all properly aligned.

📺 **sync generator**   A device used to supply a common sync signal for several sources of electrical signals. If video signals are to operate in one specific environment, they need one collective source of timing signals.

🎬 **sync mark**   A frame with a written symbol that designates the starting point of a shot or the beginning of a reel or sound track so that corresponding picture and audio may be properly synchronized.

🎬 **sync sound**   Sound recorded simultaneously with picture; also referred to as SOF (sound on film) or SOT (sound on tape).

synchronizer

🎬 An editing device that maintains several picture and sound tracks in sync during the editing process. The synchronizer consists of several sprocketed wheels, or gangs, located on a common axle (Figure 40).

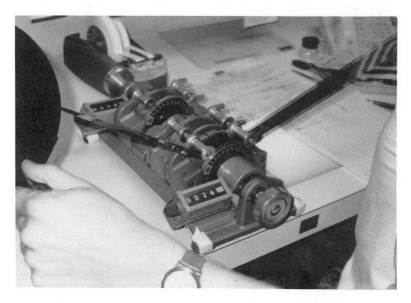

Figure 40   A film synchronizer with three gangs. Note the footage counter at the front of the synchronizer and the frame markings on two of the three gangs. Photo by Sean Sterling, courtesy of Cinema Research Corporation.

When segments of film are entered into the gangs and the gangs are locked to the axle, all segments can then be run synchronously. The synchronizer is used with rewinds in tabletop editing.

⇌ It is analogous to an editing system capable of running several sources in sync or running a video and an audio record machine in sync with each other.

☐ A device that compares incoming picture signals to a reference signal, then delays the incoming picture until it is in time with the reference signal. See also *frame synchronizer.*

T-grain™

A trademarked film and development process of the Eastman Kodak company. The T-grain is a grain of silver halide that is rectangular rather than globular. This presents a wider, flatter surface that provides thinner emulsion and more sensitivity.

The video comparison would be metal tape. The increased signal-to-noise ratio in metal tape allows for better recordings with the properly aligned recorder. SVHS, Hi8, Betacam SP, MII, D1, D2, and D3 use metal tape.

T-stop   A calibrating system for determining how much light a lens transmits to a film. Unlike F-stop calibration, which measures transmitted light only as a factor of the lens aperture, the T-stop system uses both aperture dimensions and factors of lens absorption and reflection to determine the actual amount of light that will fall on the film. T-stops offer a more accurate number at which the cinematographer can set his or her aperture. The F-stop should still be used for depth-of-field calculations. See also *F-stop*.

tail   The end of a reel or program.

tails out   A reel of videotape, audiotape, or film, where the end of the program is the first portion to be unwound and the beginning is at the center of the reel.

take

A complete shot from one camera-position angle, start to finish. Also, a take often is demarcated by the starting and stopping of film within the camera; this is true particularly when the camera position is changing during the take, as in a dolly shot. There may be several takes from one camera angle.

The video equivalent is still a take when single-camera production techniques are used. In single-camera sitcom situations, whole scenes are usually shot as one take. In many productions, there are two complete recorded versions of the performance: the dress rehearsal and the air performance.

☐ A segment of video or action defined by switching from one video source to another during a live or prerecorded live-on-tape program. Such switching generally occurs within multicamera productions.

take-up reel   The destination reel that is fed the program after viewing, editing, processing, and so on. Usually the term refers to an open reel machine; but it can also refer to a cassette machine.

☐ **tally light**   See *camera cue light.*

☐ **tape**

    1. Material onto which video or audio is recorded. See also *Mylar; oxide.*
    2. To record a signal on audio- or videotape.

tape operator

☐ A professional technician who operates a videotape machine. Some VTR operators are considered assistant editors, because, by operating the VTRs, they assist the video editor in an on-line session.

⇐ The tape operator is similar in function to an assistant editor in film. The main difference is that in video the video editor operates totally different equipment than the tape operator, somewhat hindering the upward mobility of the tape operator. On the other hand, the assistant editor is often working on the film editor's equipment and is being trained to eventually become an editor.

tape path   The physical route that the video- or audiotape travels while threaded in a machine.

tape splice   Also called **butt splice.** The joining together with transparent Mylar tape of two separate pieces of film. The pieces are joined with no overlap of frames. Since this is a temporary splice (the tape can be peeled off), this type of splice is ideal for the work-print stage of editing. The edits can be changed and rearranged without permanent damage to the print stock. The tape splice needs to be placed on both sides of an edit if the work print is to be projected. See also *splicer.*

tape splicer   See *splicer.*

target

☐ The face of a CCD or pickup tube within a video camera onto which is focused the image to be recorded.

⇐ Analogous to the film plane is that area within the film camera where the image from the lens is focused.

☐ **TBC**   See *time base corrector.*

📽 **telecine**   The machine and the process of transferring a filmed image to videotape. Top-of-the-line telecine machines are extremely expensive but very flexible in color correction and ability to handle various forms of film formats.

These most sophisticated machines use a spot of light emitted from a cathode ray tube to illuminate the film and, thus, sometimes are called flying spot scanners. The operation of this machine is left to a highly trained individual who can greatly affect the final look of the film. It is here that most of the color, density, and feel of the final product is locked onto videotape. Two other forms of telecine (of less quality and expense) that are available would be (1) a projector housed in a film chain, which has a lens focused on the face of a television camera, and (2) a video camera simply recording an image being shown on a film screen.

There are several effects that can be created in the telecine bay. Depending on the specific film-to-tape device being used, the image can be blown up (expanded) or flipped. Many telecine rooms are equipped with chromakeying capability. Often, this technique is employed to create hi-cons for later compositing in the editing bay.

☐ **TelePrompTer™**   Registered trade name for a prompting device. With typical TelePrompTers, a script is typed into a computer and then printed in large letters onto a roll of paper. This paper is then loaded onto a mechanism that transports the script at varying speeds, controlled by an operator.

In front of the television camera is a reflective screen, similar to a two-way mirror. The talent can now read the script that is reflected at him or her from the screen directly in front of the television lens. This enables the talent to both look directly into the camera and easily see the script. There is a designated person who controls the speed of the script's movement, keeping pace with the talent's reading.

Newer TelePrompTers may be more automated and computerized, eliminating the need for an operator, the roll of paper, or both.

🎥 **35-millimeter (35mm)**   The accepted standard film of the professional film industry. This film is 35 millimeters wide and has sprocket holes (perforations) running along both edges. There are approximately 16 image frames per foot of film and 4 perforations on each side per frame. Standard filming and projection rate is 24 frames per second. Although there are several alternatives (16 millimeter, Super 16, 65 millimeter, and 70 millimeter), 35 millimeter has become the most used, most suited, most supported professional format. Although this format is not the least expensive, it does offer the most complete support services.

three-stripe film

A film with three stripes of magnetic material for transfer of several tracks of audio.

A video analogy is a multitrack audiotape.

three-two pulldown   Conversion ratio pertaining to film-to-tape transferring. Since NTSC video runs at 30 frames per second and film runs at 24 frames per second, 6 video frames must be created in the film-to-tape transfer system. The most commonly used method is to repeat one field (one half of a video frame) every other frame (Figure 41). Since a frame consists of two fields, the transfer pattern becomes three fields of one frame, then two fields of the next, resulting in the term *three-two pulldown*. The *pulldown* portion of the term refers to the pulling down of the film frame into position for transfer to video. So, using simple mathematics, one video half-frame is created every 2 film frames, or a full video frame every 4 film frames. Six video frames are projected per one second of film at 24 frames per second.

Problems can arise in video effects if the three-two pulldown is not started on the same frame on both the hold-out matte *and* the foreground material (the picture being inserted in the key cut). If the pulldown is started on different frames, then there will be extra fields of the matte, whereas there are no extra fields of the insert material and vice versa, thus rendering any motion matting essentially flawed.

time base corrector (TBC)   An electronic device that corrects timing errors in video signals, errors that are normally created by fluctuations in the speed of video recorders. It is located either inside a video machine or at the output of a video machine. Most video signals from tape are

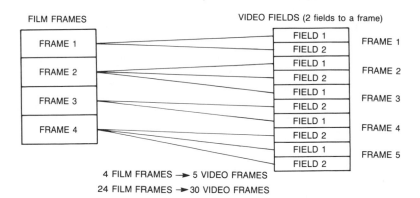

Figure 41   Three-two pulldown. During a film-to-tape transfer, in order to make 30 video frames from 24 film frames, a field is repeated every other film frame.

tremendously unstable. The TBC organizes the video signal into a viewable picture.

The TBC also provides timing adjustments so the video signal can be introduced into a switcher or other device that accepts multiple sources. The TBC stores lines of video information, which are then released in time with the rest of the video system.

One other aspect of the TBC is the ability to adjust the playback levels of the four components that comprise the video signal: setup, video level, chroma level, and hue.

time code

☐ A method of numbering, for identification and editing, every video frame with a sequential, time-based code recorded as an electronic signal on the videotape or other storage medium. Time code is read in the format of:

hours:minutes:seconds:frames

12:23:15:10

Time code is created by a time code generator. There are two types of code: non-drop frame, which is nontime accurate, and drop frame, which is accurate to real time. Time code can be recorded several ways onto videotape: on an audio track, in the vertical interval, or on an address track.

Time code is recorded in one of two manners. The first type of recording, called longitudinal recording, is digitally encoding the time code as an audio signal. The second method is recording the time code as a digitally encoded picture. This type of recording is called *vertical interval time code* (VITC). The digitally encoded signal of VITC is recorded on videotape in the vertical frame line (the vertical interval). VITC can only be recorded at the same time as the picture is being recorded.

All time code must be decoded to allow humans to decipher the code. Some audio, video, and film playback machines have time-code readers built into them. Many videotape machines do not have the ability to read vertical interval time code. Time code that is displayed in a picture *is not* time code, but a visual *representation* of the time code at that location.

Time code is usually recorded onto videotape when the original footage is recorded. However, there are occasions when footage is time coded after the production phase has been completed.

Most programs are shot with time code recorded on an audio channel or a time code channel. Then, a window dub is made. A window dub is an exact copy of the camera original, both aurally and visually, with a visual representation of time code in the picture.

Some video editors edit their shows and then manually write the time code numbers of each edit onto an edit log. Most sitcom and television shows use computer editing systems that keep a listing of each edit. This listing is used to perform the on-line, or conforming of the off-line, edit session. Time code can be placed on a tape after recording, using an audio track. See also *address track time code; longitudinal time code; vertical interval time code.*

↤ The edge numbers in film are time code's comparison. The edge numbers, copied onto the work print, are used to conform negative to work print and to keep track of footage. Another comparison, though, would be the coding of both audio and picture tracks to keep both in sync during the editing process. See also *coding.*

time code generator

▢ An electronic device that creates and records sequential, time-based numbers used to identify video frames. In video uses, the time code generator needs to be locked to either the videotape machine or the system's sync source. If the time code generator is not in time with the video or house sync, the time code recorded may be rendered useless. See also *house sync; sync generator.*

Many time code generators are also able to jam sync time code, read a code signal, and then create a new time code with the same numbers but, digitally, a new generation of signals.

↤ The film analogy would be either the machine that exposes film to the edge number during manufacturing or a coding machine that codes film and audio to help keep the two strings in sync once cutting begins.

time compress

▧ The process of accelerating real time through editorial means. The editor can, through selective elimination of action, give the appearance of an action or scene occurring faster than it would naturally. An example of time compression would be the shortening of the time it takes to walk the distance from a parked car to the front door of a house. By cutting from the car as the actor exits the vehicle to the actor approaching the front door (leaving out part of the walking), the real walking time is compressed through the use of editing.

▢ The process of slightly speeding up a program in order to shorten the program's original length. When this method is employed, the audio pitch of the program is raised slightly. There are audio machines that are capable of changing the pitch of an audio source for exactly this purpose.

timing (grading)

▧ 1. The coordination of two actions to happen at the same time. See also *back timing.*

2. The cadence of a performer when delivering a speech or line of dialogue.

The process of color balancing each individual scene of a negative. The color timer uses a machine that displays film negative on a video screen to analyze each scene. Color and exposure corrections are made for each scene and then recorded on a computer disk or paper tape. When the negative passes through the printer, the computer commands alter the light values reaching the raw print stock to achieve the required color balance.

The first timed print is called the first answer print or first approval print. It can take several attempts at timing before a totally acceptable print is realized.

In video post-production, this process would be called color correction and takes place during the conforming session called the on-line. When a production takes the time to color balance shots, it is called color correction. In its simplest form, color correction just means to adjust the four controls of the time base corrector. In more elaborate situations, a color corrector is used to adjust each shot.

In multiple video source configurations, all video sources are timed with each other. This is done by synchronizing the horizontal and subcarrier signals of an electronic device to a reference signal. A quick way to check if a source is out of horizontal timing is to perform a wipe on the switcher referenced to that timing source. A horizontal shift will occur at the end of the wipe if the source is out of horizontal timing. If the source is out of subcarrier timing, then the color will shift at the end of the wipe.

titles Words appearing in a video or film that are not an integral part of the action. Credits are a common type of title. Titles most often are created using some sort of effects. In the film process, the titles are designed at a professional title house and shot with an animation camera (Figure 42). The footage from the animation camera is then combined with the film's footage in an optical printer. The output of the optical printer is optically exposed onto raw stock.

With video, titles can be created by a title house, a character generator, or graphics system. The titles are combined with the production footage in the switcher and recorded onto a record master.

track

1. The rails on which a camera dolly rides. Similar to a small gauge railroad, these metal or wooden rails provide the smooth surface on which the dolly is mounted to provide ease of passage over uneven terrain.

2. The strings or channels of audio built on mag (film process) or on a multitrack recorder (video process). Examples could be effects, music, dialogue, narrations, or guide tracks.

tracking

Matching the position and speed of a tape to its original speed at

Figure 42   Animation stand. Also called a downshooter, this is a remote-controlled computerized camera that shoots animation, titles, and credits. Art work is placed on the stand, and the camera moves around the art work. Since the camera move is computer controlled, it can be repeated over and over, exactly the same way. Photo by Sean Sterling, courtesy of Cinema Research Corporation.

recording to produce a distortion-free playback. This is accomplished via a physical adjustment on the playback deck referencing to the control track.

➡ In film, the resolver employs a similar technique to stabilize audio playback speed. This is an audio device that constantly monitors the pulses recorded from a synchronous motor (Pilotone) and adjusts the playback to match the pulses.

🎥 **tracking shot** A shot that has camera movement in it. See also *dolly; running shot.*

🎥 **transducer** A device that converts energy of one form, such as electrical, acoustical, or mechanical, to another form. Audio and video heads and microphones, for example, are technically types of transducers.

☐ **transverse recording** The first method of video recording utilizing four video record heads and two-inch-wide videotape. The format that utilized this recording method, called quad or two-inch, is not widely used anymore.

trim

🎥 The final pass, or fine tuning, of the color of a film transfer in the telecine process.

🎬 The heads, tails, and other portions of shots that are deleted as these shots are combined in editing. Trims are set aside for future use. Longer sections are kept in trim bins. The smaller elements are stored in trim boxes.

➡ The tape process does not produce trims, so all original footage is kept during the editing process and stored on carts, on shelves, or in storage areas called vaults.

☐ **Trinitron**™ The Sony Corporation's trademark for their high-quality television picture tube that employs only one aperture grid and one electron gun. Most normal color cathode ray tubes have three electron guns, one for each of the primary light colors (red, green, and blue).

🎥 **two pop** A brief section (one or two frames) of audio placed two seconds before the start of a program; used as a synchronizing mark for film and as a cue for video programs, especially commercials.

☐ **Type C** A commonly found broadcast-quality format. Recorded onto one-inch-wide tape, there are three audio channels: two for production or editing and one for time code. This is the one-inch format that was the workhorse of the 1980s.

Entering the high-end broadcast field in the 1990s were the formats D1, D2, D3, and HDTV.

Ultimatte™

☐ A trademarked name of the Ultimatte Corporation for an advanced form of chroma key. This device is often used in television news broadcasting for compositing talent and graphics. The device is also used for creating high-contrast images (hold-out mattes) in telecine and edit bays. See also *hi-con; hold-out matte.*

⇐ The Ultimatte is analogous to a sophisticated optical printer and chroma-keying is comparable to blue-screen techniques.

ultrasonic cleaning   Cleaning film by using ultrasonic sound waves to dislodge dirt and dust from the stock. This type of cleaning is often performed before a telecine session.

undercrank

⬛ To slow down the film's speed within the camera, resulting in the speeding up of the action when the film is played at a standard rate. In production, altering the speed of the film within the camera alters the length of time the film is exposed. Either filters or iris adjustments are used to compensate for the resulting difference in light levels.

⇐ In most cases, the production video record machine's speed is not altered. Most slow-motion effects are accomplished in post-production through the use of a variable-speed tape machine or a digital disk recorder.

underscan

☐ Showing the complete picture, including the horizontal and vertical areas that are not considered "positively viewable" on a home television set. There is more picture information broadcast in a video signal than is visible on a normal home television receiver; this extra area is part contingency and part signal processing information such as vertical blanking. However, most monitors and some television sets can adjust the viewing range of the picture area. Overscanning the picture approximates the average home viewer's television.

➡ Most wide-screen formats are blowups of a 35-millimeter image with the top and bottom masked off (matted). The projecting of an unmatted wide-screen format would be similar to underscan.

upstage

1. An originally theatrical production term meaning movement away from the audience, toward the back of the stage. The term is also used in sitcom productions, as such programs often are performed much like a play.

2. An acting term indicating that one actor, by means other than dialogue or planned action, draws attention from the intended center of attention to himself or herself.

Ursa™   Trade name of recently developed and marketed film-to-tape telecine machine. See also *flying spot scanner; Rank Cintel; telecine.*

variable-speed playback

A video playback machine with the capability of maintaining image stability while displaying video at a speed faster or slower than sound speed. Most variable-speed tape machines are capable of one times reverse to three times sound speed. Some expensive digital disk recorders are capable of –30 to +30 times sound speed.

An optical printer creates the variable-speed effects through step printing. See also *effects; optical printer.*

vault   A storage area specifically built for video or film. Both mediums require dry cool areas for long-term storage. However, many facilities store their footage in a room that is simply kept at room temperature because the film or tape moves in and out regularly. Nevertheless, this temporary storage area, even though it is not totally climate-controlled, is still called a vault.

VCR   See *videocassette recorder.*

vectorscope   An oscilloscope (CRT-based display) used for monitoring phase and saturation of color within a video signal. The vectorscope also is used to time video signals to each other. See also *blanking.*

vertical interval   A period of time during the video-imaging process when the scanning beam within a picture tube resets itself between fields of information. While the beam resets, image information is suppressed. During this time, which lasts as long as 21 lines, other (nonimage) information can be inserted, including, but not limited to, closed captioning information (CC), vertical interval time code (VITC), vertical interval test signal (VITS), and vertical interval reference signal (VIRS). See also *blanking; scanning.*

vertical interval recording   During the time that the video signal is blanked out between fields, other signals can be inserted within the video signal. The equivalent of 21 lines of information are blanked in the time that it takes the electron beam to return to the top of the screen. Some of these lines are used to encode standard reference signals within the television signal. See also *closed captioning; vertical interval reference signal; vertical interval test signal; vertical interval time code.*

vertical interval reference signal (VIRS)   An encoded signal used as a reference signal for automatic color correction circuitry in the television set. It is recorded on lines 19 and 20 of the video signal.

vertical interval test signal (VITS)   A series of test signals used to judge a video system's recording capability.

vertical interval time code (VITC)   A digitally encoded visual signal that can be recorded on lines 12 and 14 of the video signal. A special device is required to read or write time code within the vertical interval.

video assist   A system of recording a video image from a film camera, the same image that has been used to expose the film. The system operates by either recording the ground-glass image of the camera viewfinder or splitting off a portion of the light after it passes through the lens but before it exposes the film. This video footage can be used as preliminary editing footage or simply as a check for framing, focus, performance, and so on.

video black   See *edit black.*

video disk   A type of optical disk, a platter-like recording medium, that has picture and audio information recorded onto it. Originally, video disks were a read-only medium; the recording process was too difficult for users to employ. However, recent developments have brought read-and-write capabilities to video disks, which makes them more attractive in general and specifically for video random-access editing.

video master   See *edited master.*

video projector

A device that projects a video picture onto a screen, as opposed to displaying it in a CRT. Although the home units are still not of the best quality, there are several very expensive video projectors that are impressive.

Although the video projector is compared to a film projector, the quality of image in the film domain still is far better than video projection.

video tap   The port or output where a video assist image is brought out of the film camera. See also *video assist.*

videocassette recorder (VCR)   Usually referring to a tape machine that only accepts cassettes, like a three-quarter-inch, Betamax, Betacam, or VHS reel machine. An open reel machine is often referred to as VTR (video tape recorder).

videotape A strong thin backing covered with a highly magnetic substance used to record or play back video signals through the use of a videotape recorder or player.

videotape recorder (VTR) Usually referring to an open reel machine, as opposed to a VCR, a videocassette recorder.

viewfinder An optical- or video-based system that enables a film- or video-camera operator to see the image being recorded. The term *viewfinder* is most commonly used to describe a tubelike optical scope immediately accessing image-laden light from within a camera.

VIRS See *vertical interval reference signal.*

VITC See *vertical interval time code.*

VITS See *vertical interval test signal.*

VO See *voice over.*

voice-over (VO) A narrator's audio, used mainly in documentaries and commercials. A voice-over can be a temporary scratch track or the final audio used for presentation.

volume unit (VU) A measure of sound, often displayed on a VU meter. One volume unit is the equivalent to one decibel. The VU meter is a universal measuring device for audio recording in the audio, film, and broadcasting business.

VTR See videotape recorder.

VU See *volume unit.*

VU meter A device that measures loudness of an audio signal. Zero on the VU meter is a universal standard. See also *decibel; volume unit.*

wall-to-wall   Audio or picture term meaning full. A show that is full of visual effects would be said to contain wall-to-wall effects. A program that had effects, music, dialogue, and voice over throughout would have wall-to-wall audio.

warning bell   A bell that sounds on the set and outside the studio at the beginning and at the end of a shot; designed to caution people that a scene is being shot and to keep noise to a minimum. See also *bells on/ bells off.*

waveform monitor   An oscilloscope used to display video, chroma, and sync levels. The waveform monitor has a series of different display functions and is always near professional video equipment. See also *blanking.*

weaving   Also called **film weave**. The slight side-to-side rocking of film as it travels through the gate in the projector. Film weave usually goes unnoticed until there is some completely still image (like a video title) that highlights the film's motion. Since the video characters are basically motionless, the rocking motion of the film becomes very apparent.

There are several types of physical or electronic devices that can be employed in a film-to-tape (videotape) transfer that can eliminate film weave during the transfer. All must take place during the film transfer process.

wet gate

A printing mechanism that surrounds a film with a liquid during exposure in order to minimize light refraction resulting from scratches or other damage to the film's surface (Figure 43).

The video equivalent is a dropout compensator, an electronic device that senses a lack of oxide on a playback tape and repeats previous video information in that damaged area of picture.

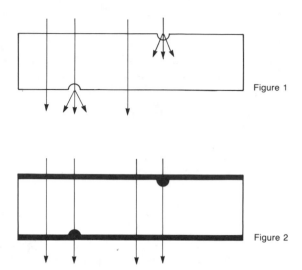

Figure 1

Figure 2

Figure 43   Wet gate operation. The wet gate helps avoid light refraction by optically filling surface damage.

white balance

☐ The circuit in a video camera that, when engaged, automatically detects and adjusts for differences in color temperature. By placing a white piece of material in front of the camera at a shooting location and engaging the *white balance* button, the camera adjusts itself to the light on the white material.

⇐ Film does not have an automatic device to compensate for color temperature. The process in film is to light a subject and then to use color-correction lenses to correct for minor variations in light-source color temperature and the intended exposure color temperature as specified by the film manufacturer. If the lighting is far from the film's specification, then color-compensator lenses are used to drastically alter the light reaching the film stock.

white level

☐ A term referring to a video signal without chroma (color) information; often checked on the IRE scale as displayed on a waveform monitor. The white levels should not exceed 104 percent of white; if they do, they can cause technical problems in the recording process.

⇐ The film comparison would be the shoulder of a film stock's characteristic curve, that level at which the film is totally exposed with no tonal differentiation.

wide-screen   Indicating any film format that has a screen ratio greater than that of academy standard (1.33:1).

wild track (wild line)   Audio that is recorded without accompanying picture. When recording wild lines in film production, the camera is not rolled. A wild line can also be recorded without any cameras present, such as in an audio studio.

window dub

☐ A video copy of original camera footage with time code numbers burned into the image. A window dub is made either during production or after shooting is completed. Most window dubs are on three-quarter-inch or half-inch home-consumer formats and are used for viewing or editing off-line. Since window dubs have the time code permanently burned into the picture, it is of little use in the editing of final program, except as a reference copy.

⇌ Film work print is an equivalent to the window dub. The film editor edits with work print. The video editor works with window dubs. The main conceptional difference between the two is that the video window dub also has production audio recorded on it.

wipe   A transition between two pictures using a geometrical design. The edge of the wipe can be hard-edged or soft-edged and can be colored. Common wipes are a single vertical line, a single horizontal line, and a circle.

In film, the wipe is performed by the optical printer and its adjustable shutters, which expose raw stock to an image of other film sources.

In video, the switcher performs the wipe from A and B source reels.

wireless microphone   A microphone that uses radio waves, rather than wires, to transmit the sound to the mixer or audio recorder.

work print

1. An exact copy of camera original footage with corresponding key numbers used to create a program. In the finishing process, the camera original is conformed to the edited program created by cutting the work print.

⇌ The video window dub is the equivalent to film work print; however, the window dub has a copy of production audio on it as well as picture.

2. The actual edited product composed of work print and audio track is also called a work print.

⇌ Work print used in this fashion would be the video equivalent of an off-line or rough cut.

work light   Lights that have no real production purpose other than general illumination. See also *houselights.*

wow   Audio distortion caused by variation of speeds in playback speed.

wrap

A term indicating the end of a production or session: "That's a wrap."

The circular tape path around the rotating drum of a videotape machine.

x A mark drawn on work print and corresponding audio track; used to indicate sync on both the picture and sound track.

xlr A type of audio connector that comes in male and female configurations. There are three prongs or three receptors housed in a metal cylinder.

☐ **y** Symbol for the luminance (amount of white) portion of a color television signal. When combined with R – Y (red minus luminance) and B – Y (blue minus luminance), the three signals are the ones used in creating the component (three wires) video path. D1, MII, and Betacam are component recording formats. See also *formats*.

y/c

☐ Symbol for luminance separated from chroma (color) information; a type of recording used in Super VHS, VHS, Hi8, and 8-millimeter recordings.

⇌ Compared to film, the formats of 8 millimeter and super 8 would compare to the Y/C recording process.

zoom The expanding of an image. A zoom can be accomplished in several ways. In production, using a zoom lens is a common method of expanding an image. In film post-production, the optical printer can create a zoom. In video post-production, a digital video effects device can create the zoom. In film-to-tape transferring, the telecine device can zoom into an image.

zoom lens A lens with movable elements that allow the lens to change its focal length. A zoom lens usually needs more light (it is a slower lens) than a fixed lens. A zoom lens is usually less clear than a fixed lens because of the numerous lenses involved.